PLUG IN

TO THE POWER OF GOD

STEVE INK

WESTBOW
PRESS®
A DIVISION OF THOMAS NELSON
& ZONDERVAN

WestBow Press books may be ordered through booksellers or by contacting:

WestBow Press
A Division of Thomas Nelson & Zondervan
1663 Liberty Drive
Bloomington, IN 47403
www.westbowpress.com
1 (866) 928-1240

ISBN: 978-1-9736-6998-2 (sc)
ISBN: 978-1-9736-7000-1 (hc)
ISBN: 978-1-9736-6999-9 (e)

Library of Congress Control Number: 2019910888

Print information available on the last page.

WestBow Press rev. date: 08/28/2019

Thanks
To those of you who reviewed the manuscript
and made helpful suggestions for this book.

To Bruce and Sharon for help with the pictures.
To Angela, Randy, Janelle, Gordon, and Sharon for help with the text.

www.steveink.net

Contents

ABBREVIATIONS

Old Testament

Genesis (Ge)

Exodus (Ex)

Leviticus (Lev)

Numbers (Nu)

Deuteronomy (Dt)

Joshua (Jos)

Judges (Jdg)

Ruth (Ru)

1 Samuel (1Sa)

2 Samuel (2Sa)

1 Kings (1Ki)

2 Kings (2 Ki)

1 Chronicles (1Ch)

2 Chronicles (2Ch)

Ezra (Ezr)

Nehemiah (Ne)

Esther (Est)

Job (Job)

Psalms (Ps)

Ecclesiastes (Ecc)

Song of Songs (SS)

Isaiah (Isa)

Jeremiah (Jer)

Lamentations (La)

Ezekiel (Eze)

Daniel (Da)

Hosea (Hos)

Joel (Joel)

Amos (Am)

Obadiah (Ob)

Jonah (Jnh)

Micah (Mic)

Nahum (Na)

Habakkuk (Hab)

Zephaniah (Zep)

Haggai (Hag)

Zechariah (Zec)

Malachi (Mal)

New Testament

Matthew (Mt)

Mark (Mk)

Luke (Lk)

John (Jn)

Ephesians (Eph)

Philippians (Php)

Colossians (Col)

1Thessalonians (1Th)

Hebrews (Heb)

James (Jas)

1 Peter (1Pe)

2 Peter (2Pe)

Acts (Ac)	2Thessalonians (2Th)	1 John (1Jn)
Romans (Ro)	1 Timothy (1Ti)	2 John (2Jn)
1 Corinthians (1Co)	2 Timothy (2Ti)	3 John (3Jn)
2 Corinthians (2Co)	Titus (Tit)	Jude (Jude)
Galatians (Gal)	Philemon (Phm)	Revelation (Rev)

All biblical quotes are taken from the *New International Version*, software by WORDsearch 11, Powered by Lifeway 2017.

The phrase "emphasis added" has not been used here when there are italicized words in a biblical quote. Take note that any italicizing of a biblical quote is adding emphasis.

BCE: Before Common Era (corresponding to the former use of BC)
CE: Common (or Christian) Era (corresponding to the former use of AD)

PREFACE

A Powerful Computer

Imagine buying a brand-new, high-powered laptop computer. It is advertised as having a long battery life, solid internet and wi-fi connections, and the capability of running multiple programs simultaneously without noticeably slowing down processing speeds. This computer can do complicated math computations, create powerful audio and video files, provide you with tools for creative and technical writing, grant you access to a world of internet research, and significantly enhance your gifts so you can effectively accomplish all kinds of activities.

You've seen the promotional material on this computer and are excited by what it can do. You smile as you take it out of the box. You remove the plastic wrapping and connect the cables to the printer, carefully following the instructions. And then you push the power button.

Nothing happens. You push the power button again. Still nothing. What's wrong with this computer? It should work. You've followed all the instructions to a T. They advertised this laptop as an amazing tool that will enhance your life and work. Did you get sold a bill of goods?

So you call technical support.

"Hello, what can I do for you?"

"Well, I just bought this new computer. It's supposed to do all kinds of wonderful things, but nothing happens when I push the power button."

The tech support person asks, "Is the computer plugged in?"

"Well, no. Isn't it supposed to have a long-lasting battery?"

"But did you charge the battery first?"

"No, I thought it came charged."

"Sometimes they do, but I suggest that you plug the computer in and see how it works."

You pull out the plug, connect the computer to the outlet, let it charge a bit, and then push the power button. It takes a little while as the computer needs to store enough power to be able to run the programs. The computer then makes its opening sound, the screen lights up, and the programs begin to load. In no time at all, the computer is up and running with all the bells and whistles that were advertised. You sheepishly realize, *I guess I just needed to plug in.*

Plugging In

Every electronic device needs to be plugged in at some point. My wide-screen TV, toaster, lamps, hair dryer, refrigerator, and vacuum require a direct connection to the outlet. If the device is not plugged in, it will not run at all. Other devices like my cell phone and cameras run on batteries. Batteries may last for hours, days, or perhaps longer. However, all batteries run out of power eventually. Then it is time to replace the battery or recharge them to get the equipment running again.

Sometimes devices can run off either power taken directly from the outlet or from the battery. While plugged in, some devices can run with the battery charging at the same time. My laptop works like this, as does my electric razor and my cell phone. Technology has just recently introduced wireless charging, but there is still a charging process.

Even solar devices are plugged in—to the sun. We place solar collector panels on our rooftops or on the ground facing in the direction that will maximize their exposure to sunlight. We store the power collected from the sun in batteries so that power can be provided when the sun is not available. But sooner or later, the collectors need to be able to see the sun or they will not be able to draw power from the source.

No matter what type of electrical device we try to use, it has to be plugged in to a power source sooner or later or it will not operate.

Plugging into God

The same principle applies in our relationship with God. People will tell you how wonderful God is, how much he can do for you, and the power that comes from being connected to him, but we do have to connect. Instead of being plugged into the sun as solar collectors are, we need to be plugged in to the *Son*—the Son of God—as the incarnation of[1] and access to God.[2] Without this recharging and empowering, we will spiritually lose strength and die.[3]

Our spiritual plug can be compared to a three-pronged plug commonly found in the United States. The ground prong is frequent (daily) study of the Bible. The second prong is daily (constant) prayer. The third prong is regular fellowship (partnership) with other Christians. The receptacle into which we plug our three-prong plug is Jesus. When all three prongs are plugged in and functioning, God's Spirit, as the current of life, will freely flow back and forth, complete the circuit in a safe way, and provide the power we need to be the people God wants us to be. It is the three prongs of the plug that open our hearts to the leading of God's Spirit, which fills us and empowers us.

This book will not explore the likeness of Jesus to an electrical appliance receptacle, except to say that our connection to God comes through Jesus Christ (Jn.10:7; 14:6; Ac.4:13) like electrical power comes through the receptacle. The discussion in this book will focus on the three prongs of the spiritual plug and on the powerful current that runs through that plug.

Admittedly, this image of a three-prong plug with current is an oversimplification of the process of how God's power is poured out on his people. You don't want to overanalyze each component of the image as it is not meant to be a true parallel in all the detail. However, this image is a bit like a parable that hits at the core of an essential truth. As such, it has real value in helping us understand how to access the power of God.

---

[1] *The Son as the incarnation of God.* Mt.1:23; Jn.1:1–3, 14; 8:58; 10:30; 17:5; Col.2:9–10; Php.2:5–11; Heb.1:2–3.

[2] *The Son is the access to God.* Jn.10:7; 14:6; Ac.4:13.

[3] *Lose strength and die.* The question has been raised as to whether any divine life can remain in a person who has made a commitment to God through Christ but not plugged in to God for some time. The Bible does not directly answer this question. However, there are a number of passages that indicate failing to continue on with God through Christ can be spiritually fatal (Ro.11:22; 1Co.9:27; Gal.5:4; Heb.2:1; 6:4; 10:26; Ja.5:9; 2Pe.2:20). It is those who persevere who find the life God offers (Col.1:22–23; Heb.3:6). In fact, faith without action is dead (Ja.2:14–19). God has called us to plug in as you will see through the following chapters.

Part One

THE GROUND PRONG
FREQUENT (DAILY) BIBLE STUDY

All Scripture is God-breathed and is useful for teaching, rebuking, correcting and training in righteousness, so that the servant of God may be thoroughly equipped for every good work. (2Tim.3:16–17)

CHAPTER ONE

Nature of the Bible

My First Bible

I was given my first Bible as a child. It was an inexpensive, black-covered King James Version with all the seventeenth-century archaic language that a grade school child of the twentieth century could not possibly understand. It had red edges on the pages and print that was much smaller than I was used to. It didn't have any pictures. Surprisingly though, I thought it was special. Although I didn't read much of it, I treasured that inexpensive Bible for many years.

It was a special gift because it came from my grandmother. She had been active in church throughout her life. She played piano and organ for her church. She appeared to me to be the spiritual leader of her family. While I was still young, she began sharing with me the importance of God and his Bible. She explained that it held the words of God. She took me to my first wedding so I could experience a *Christian* wedding.

Grandma was not pushy. She did not try to convert me to one particular denomination. I don't remember her ever chastising me or anyone in my family for not going to church on a regular basis. She simply shared tidbits of information about God and his Word that began to shape my thinking. I don't remember her teaching any specific dogma or tenants of faith. But her sharing began to create in me a respect for God and his Word, the Bible.

The First Prong

The first prong in that three-pronged plug that allows us to plug into God is Bible study. It is the *ground* plug. The ground plug, which is the largest of the three, is there to keep us safe. The idea behind grounding in an electrical apparatus is to protect the people who use metal-encased equipment from electric shock. The ground plug is connected directly to the casing. Although the equipment may work without a ground prong, there is danger that the hot wire will come loose, make contact with the casing, and surprise whoever handles the casing with a serious or even fatal shock. The ground plug protects against this.

The Bible serves as the ground plug in our spiritual lives. It is our baseline and primary source to learn about and be reminded of the nature of God and what he wants of us. It keeps us safe and secure from the constantly moving tides of human culture like a ground plug of an electrical appliance protects us from shock. Without it, we could easily be swayed by ineffective philosophies or dangerous heresies that lead us down rabbit holes instead of along the path to abundant life. We might find ourselves lacking certainty as to what God actually wants. The Bible's guiding principles pull us back to the truth and actuality of life. The Bible provides us with direction toward the full and amazing life that only God can offer.

The Berean church of the first century CE is upheld as a model of how we should use scripture to test and determine whether a new teaching is actually from God or not. This was a first-century church in the city of Berea, now called Veria, in Greek Macedonia in northern Greece. The apostle Paul and his companion, Silas, took a new message to the Bereans.

> As soon as it was night, the believers sent Paul and Silas away to Berea. On arriving there, they went to the Jewish synagogue. Now the Berean Jews were of more noble character than those in Thessalonica, for they received the message with great eagerness and examined the Scriptures every day to see if what Paul said was true. (Ac.17:10–11)

This ground plug (Bible study) ensures that teaching that is contrary to God's written Word won't carry us away. We test the teaching with the principles established in the Bible. If the new teaching is contrary, it must be rejected. This testing of a new message by the biblical standard is essential to one's spiritual health.

A Unique Book

The Bible is the best-selling book of all time. It has been translated into more languages than any other book. About half the world's population call some or all of it "scripture" or "God's Word."[4] No other book in history has come close to the circulation and impact of the Bible.

The Bible is God's Word as communicated through human authors. It is deemed the result of special divine revelation. Scripture is the result of God communicating to people in several ways (Ex.19:16–18; 31:18; 1Ki.19:11–13; Da.5:5–7; Jer.1:9; 36:17–18; Lk.1:1–4; Rev.9:17). Although we tend to think of the term *prophecy* as referring to a foretelling of the future, in the ancient world, the basic meaning of prophecy had to do with *proclaiming* the Word of God, not foretelling the future. God was at work through his Spirit in this proclamation. "For prophecy never had its origin in the will of man, but men spoke from God as they were carried along by the Holy Spirit" (2Pe.1:21).

Picking the Right Bible

Today, portions of the Bible have been translated into thousands of languages.

> As of October 2017, the full Bible has been translated into 670 languages, the New Testament has been translated into 1,521 languages, and Bible portions or stories have been translated into 1,121 other languages. Thus, at least

---

[4] *Followers.* Three religious groups, accounting for about half the world's population, view parts or all of the Bible as scripture. Jews accept the Old Testament ("Hebrew Bible" or "Tanakh" to the Jews), Christians accept the Old and New Testaments, and Muslims accept the Old and New Testaments and Koran as scripture.

some portion of the Bible has been translated into 3,312 languages.[5]

Even in English, there are myriad translations. They range from more literal word-for-word translations (which tend to be awkward to read but protect the original author's phraseology) to loose paraphrases (which provide an easy-to-read modern translation but may compromise some of the integrity of the original text). When I became a Christian in college, I decided I would try to collect all the contemporary English translations. There weren't that many when I began my Christian walk. I compared various translations and personally found that there were very few substantive differences in meaning.[6]

So how do you pick a translation? It depends on your purpose as a reader.[7] If you want a Bible for general reading, you will probably want one that uses common English thoughts and phrases and perhaps even a paraphrase. If you want to delve into the text to study the terms and phrases as they were originally written, you probably want a more literal translation. Or you could pick something in the middle, like a dynamic equivalent that tries to maintain the author's original phrases and grammar except where it is misleading in our modern world. In this book, I've quoted verses from the New International Version (NIV), which is considered one of those dynamic equivalent translations.

---

[5] *Bible Translations*, online at https://en.wikipedia.org/wiki/Bible_translations. *How We Got the Bible* (Torrance: Rose Publishing, 2005), slide 19, states portions of the Bible have been translated into at least 2,426 languages. Whatever the actual number, it is a lot!

[6] *Translation Differences.* I did once have a copy of a hippie version of the New Testament with language like "keep on trucking with Jesus" and other colloquial phrases, which was clearly a paraphrase. But I did not find the meaning substantially different than the more literal translations. For more on translations read *The Challenge of Bible Translation,* editors Glen G. Scorgie, Mark L. Strauss, and Steven M. Voth (Grand Rapids: Zondervan, 2003).

[7] Gordon D. Fee and Douglas Stuart, in their *How to Read the Bible for All Its Worth* (Grand Rapids: Zondervan, 2014), suggest it is good to have one primary middle-type translation that you compare to others to get a better feel for the message of the original author.

Don't Believe Everything People Tell You

Although scholars tend to agree on the authenticity of the documents making up most of the Bible, some will try to convince you that the Bible couldn't be what it proclaims. They will challenge the dates, the style of writing, events described, and even the authorship of the documents.

I attended a secular state university for my undergraduate studies. I took every religious study and Bible course the school offered. I'll never forget the day when one of my Bible course professors told us the New Testament could not have been written by the apostles because it wasn't written until the last half of the second century CE. This was coming from a respected college professor. We were sitting in his class to learn from him because he knew more than we did. As we left the class that day, a fellow Christian student lamented, "He just destroyed my faith."

I decided I would do some research to see if what he said was true. The first thing I discovered is that the earliest physical *copy* of part of the New Testament in existence is a section of the Gospel of John known as a part of the John Rylands Fragments.[8] This copy, dubbed P52 and generally dated the first half of the second century,[9] was perhaps written only thirty years after the apostle John completed writing the original. This fragment, along with other early fragments, is being kept at the John Rylands University Library in Manchester, England. The Gospel of John could not have been written in the late second century or later if we have a physical copy of a portion of the Gospel of John dated the first half of the second century.

As I continued my research, I found that the writings of early Christian writers, such as Clement of Rome (circa 95 CE),[10] the pseudo Barnabas

---

[8] *Copy.* Archaeologists do not believe we have found any of the original documents of either the thirty-nine books of the Old Testament or twenty-seven books of the New Testament. However, we have found thousands of ancient copies and translations. It may be that the originals, used as masters for copies, may have simply worn out over time.

[9] *P52.* Bruce Manning Metzger, *The Text of the New Testament* (New York & Oxford: Oxford University Press, 1968), 38–39.

[10] *1 Clement.* Chpt.2 – Titus 3:1, Acts 20:35, Chpt.7 – 1 Pet 3:20, 2 Pet 2:5, Chpt.9 – Heb 11:5, Chpt.34 – Quotes 1 Cor 2:9 and calls it scripture, Chpt.35 – Rom 1:32, Chpt.36 – Heb 1:3–4, Chpts.37 and 38 – Church as a body metaphor, as in 1 Corinthians, Chpt.46 – James 4:1, Chpt.46 – Jesus's "millstone" quote (which is

writings (circa 100 CE), Ignatius (110),[11] Polycarp (110–150),[12] Hermas (115–140), the Didache (120–150), Papias (130–140), Diognetus (150), and Justin Martyr (150), all appear to quote numerous sections of the New Testament or actually reference the New Testament documents themselves. All these examples are evidence that the documents were written prior to the second half of the second century CE. Clement's writings indicate the New Testament documents were clearly written in the first century CE.

I then discovered that almost all scholars (both religious and secular) believe Galatians, Romans, and 1 and 2 Corinthians were written by the Paul, who lived in the first century. The grammar is what we would expect of Paul and is so consistent that scholars use these four documents to determine if other writings are Paul's. These documents were written as if one had been in Paul's situation with real emotions flaring up (unlike a hypothetical detached writer who was pretending to be Paul years later). Additionally, Peter[13] and Luke[14] (who we believe wrote in the first century) both make reference to Paul's writings. All this evidence was compelling for a first-century writing of the New Testament documents.

What I discovered in my research was that some scholars (a very few) didn't *think* the documents were written in the first century because we don't have physical originals dated from the first century. They *presumed*

---

present in Matthew, Mark and Luke), Chpt.49 – James 5:20. *Witness of the Early Church Writers*, online at http://www.datingthenewtestament.com/Fathers.htm.

[11] *Ignatius.* Letter to the Ephesians Chpt.2 – John 8:29, Chpt.3 – John 17:11–12, Chpt.5 – James 4:6, Chpt.6 – names Onesimus, as in Philemon, Chpt.6 – John 1:14, Chpt.7 – 1 Tim 4:10, Chpt.8 – 1 Pet 2:9, Chpt.9 – Matt 5:2, 2 Tim 2:24–25, Luke 23:34, Chpt.11 – Rom 2:4, Chpt.12 – Matt 23:35, Acts 9:15, Chpt.13 – Eph 6:16, 6:12, Chpt.14 – Luke 10:27, Matt 12:33, Chpt.15 – 1 Cor 4:20, Rom 10:10, 2 Cor 8:18, Chpt.16 – 2 Cor 6:14-16, Chpt.18 – 1 Cor 1:20, Letter to the Magnesians Chpt.3 – 1 Tim 4:12, Chpt.4 – Luke 6:46, Chpt.8 – 2 Cor 5:17, mentions Judaizers, Chpt.9 – 2 Thess 3:10, Phil 3:18–19, 2 Tim 3:4, Chpt.10 – Acts 11:2, Letter to the Trallians, Chpt.9 – Heb 10:12–13, Chpt.11 – warns of "Nicolaitanes," Letter to the Romans, Chpt.2 – 2 Cor 4:18, Chpt.7 – Gal 2:20, Letter to the Philadelphians, Chpt.2 – 2 Tim 3:6, Chpt.6 – "dragon Nicolaitanes, Letter to the Smyrnans, Chpt.3 – Maybe Rev 1:7. *Witness of the Early Church Writers*, Ibid.

[12] *Polycarp. Letter of Polycarp to the Philippians* ch.1. p.33 quotes Ac.2:24a. Ch.2 p.33 quotes all of Mt.7:1 & Lk.6:36. Ch.5.p.34 quotes a portion of Galatians 6:7.

[13] 2Pe.3:15–16.

[14] 1Ti.5:18 & Lk.10:7.

that Christianity hadn't developed that far during the first century. But it is important to remember that we don't have any originals of Julius Caesar's writings on the Gallic Wars, or of the sayings of Plato, Socrates, or Aristotle. The oldest documents or copies of documents that contain these writings are dated long after the deaths of the authors. Yet there is general consensus that Caesar wrote or directed the writing of the Gallic Wars, and that Plato, Socrates, and Aristotle were actually the authors of the sayings ascribed to them. The lack of authenticated originals from the authors' days does not hinder such belief. I could find no archeological, linguistic, or historical data to lead to the conclusion that the New Testament documents were written any later than the first century.[15] Rather than shaking my faith, the professor had strengthened it and my belief that the New Testament is what it reports to be—the Word of God spoken through people of the first century CE.

If you find someone questioning a traditional perspective to the Bible, take some time to research the issue yourself. The traditional viewpoint is often the most commonly accepted viewpoint because of the facts that support it. Of course, widespread acceptance of a viewpoint doesn't necessarily mean it is right. But the "knowledgeable" professor could also be wrong.

The Bible as God's Word

When speaking of biblical inspiration, the term "inspiration" has a different meaning from the way we often use the word when someone gets a great idea or the source of artistic expression. In the Bible, the prophet or writer is communicating the words or concepts that have come to him or her through God's communications. It is inspiration by *revelation*, not inspiration by *imagination*.

The Bible speaks about its own power and effect on the human life. This is not just another ancient manuscript. It has power in the lives of its readers. The prophet Isaiah wrote, "So is my word that goes out from my

---

[15] *Later Additions.* There do appear to be later additions to the original New Testament documents, like Mark 16:9–30 and John 7:53–8:11, as these are not found in the earliest copies of the documents. But this does not affect the integrity of the original writings.

mouth: It will not return to me empty, but will accomplish what I desire and achieve the purpose for which I sent it" (Isa.55:11). The author of the letter to the Hebrews discerned the power of God's word sharing, "the word of God is living and active. Sharper than any double-edged sword, it penetrates even to dividing soul and spirit, joints and marrow; it judges the thoughts and attitudes of the heart" (Heb.4:12).

This dynamic effect on human life may explain why the Bible has been so popular, so attacked, and so dynamic in the lives of people across the globe for thousands of years. It is God's Word, capable of helping us connect to him and plug into that power that can only come from God.

A Light to Guide

Psalm 119 is the longest chapter in the Bible and focuses on the nature of the Word of God and how it is meant to be a guide in our lives. The author writes, "Your word is a lamp to my feet and a light for my path" (Ps.119:105). The Bible is like a lamp, or in modern terminology, like a flashlight or headlamp.

I think of the many nights I have spent at campsites in Yosemite National Park, Hume Lake, or Daybreak Camp in Felton, California. It is very helpful to have a flashlight at nighttime. There have been times when I have found myself trying to navigate these campsites at night without a flashlight and it is not easy. I may stumble and trip over rocks, logs, or ditches. I may have trouble figuring out in which direction I should try to move because I can't see the path and I'm not exactly sure how to navigate to my end destination. I can get hurt trying to move through these dark places without a flashlight.

A flashlight does not show me what is a mile down the path. It only lights the path a few steps ahead of where I am. It gives just enough light to help me take the next few steps safely. The Bible works like this. I can't see what will happen in this physical life ten years in the future by reading the Bible. But it does give guidance to help me know how to take the next few steps in the here and now.

When I find myself in a moral dilemma, in which two forces are tugging on me to move in different directions, the Bible provides me with the spiritual principles to help me know which way I should go. I see more clearly.

Now, after I have used the flashlight a number of times to make it from my campsite to a particular destination, my dependence on the flashlight decreases. I start to learn the path, where the rocks and logs are hiding, and how to make the trek safely in the dark. In the same way, after using the Bible repeatedly to deal with a certain type of issue, the teaching has been imprinted on my soul. I don't need to pull out my Bible again and again as a guide each time I am confronted with a decision because the Word of God has become a part of me. James says it this way, "Humbly accept the word *planted* in you, which can save you" (Ja.1:21).

The Word is planted in our souls by repeated use and consideration. When it is planted, it is solidly in place and cannot be easily pulled up. It is there when I need it to protect and guide me. It's a light from within.

Don't Ignore It

We are warned not to read the Word of God and then ignore it. James points out that it would be like looking in a mirror and then refusing to do anything to change your appearance and thus losing the value of the mirror.

> Do not merely listen to the word, and so deceive yourselves. Do what it says. Anyone who listens to the word but does not do what it says is like a man who looks at his face in a mirror and, after looking at himself, goes away and immediately forgets what he looks like. But the man who looks intently into the perfect law that gives freedom, and continues to do this, not forgetting what he has heard, but doing it – he will be blessed in what he does. (Ja.1:21–25)

I remember the Fonz in the old TV series *Happy Days* set in the 1950s. A cool teenager, Fonz, would swagger up before a mirror, pull out his comb, look at himself in the mirror, and decide nothing more was needed. He would put his comb away without ever touching his hair. It was as if he was saying, "My hair is perfect, and I don't need to do anything to change it."

In our spiritual lives, we know that we need to change. Every one of us needs to change. The Bible says, "There is none righteous, no not one" (Ro.3:10). "All of us fall short of the glory of God" (Ro.3:23). "If we say we have no sin, then we deceive ourselves" (1Jn.1:8). All of us have the need for improvement and growth. Thus, when we look into the mirror of the Bible's message, we all need to actually use the comb to change what is out of place.

Have you ever been surprised by the way you look in the mirror? Perhaps you come inside from a windy day. Maybe you take a quick look after eating a messy meal. You looked at the mirror and your eyes open wide. *Oh, if only I had known I had that smudge of dirt on my forehead. I didn't realize my eyes looked so baggy! Where did that cowlick come from? Wish someone had told me one eyebrow went up and the other down! Where did I pick up that mustard stain on my shirt?*

God is trying to shape us into who we can be. This shaping is a lifelong process of looking into the mirror of the Bible and allowing God to gradually change us into the people of God that we can become. We look into the Bible, see what needs changing, and adjust the way we live life. It's looking at ourselves honestly.

Identifying Areas That Need Change

The Bible helps us identify areas in our lives that need change. It can help us identify sin (which is harmful and destructive) and godliness (which is healing and helpful). Sometimes our own culture promotes life choices that are destructive and deemed sinful by God. The apostle Paul warns, "Do not conform any longer to the pattern of this world, but be transformed by the renewing of your mind. Then you will be able to test and approve what God's will is—his good, pleasing and perfect will" (Ro.12:2).

The entertainment industry in the United States is constantly pushing our moral boundaries of sexual propriety. Day after day, show after show, movie after movie, book after book, we are exposed to primary characters who engage in sexual behavior that is considered sinful and harmful in the Bible. God is trying to keep us out of harm's way. The enticement can be strong, especially when our culture accepts it. But we are not to conform to the ever-changing culture of the day regarding the timeless principles of sexual purity. We are his—not the world's. God calls us to a higher standard of sexual purity (Eph.5:3).

Our culture may neglect the poor, discriminate against a race of people, or disparage some other group that does not have the natural clout to force us to address their concerns. We are to be impartial and not favor one economic or racial group of people over another. The Bible teaches us to look out for the poor, the widowed, the orphans, and the oppressed. God calls us to a higher standard of social justice (Isa.1:17; Mic.6:8; Mt.7:12; Ja.1:27).

The Word of God Is Food for the Soul

Our physical bodies need tangible food to survive. So too our spiritual bodies need spiritual nourishment. The Bible is spiritual food. Jesus said, "Man does not live on bread alone but on every word that comes from the mouth of the Lord" (quote of Dt.8:3 found in Lk.4:4).

We need the right kind of food for the body. Howard Hughes, one of the wealthiest men on earth before he died in 1976, was malnourished because he ate cookies and not a balanced diet. He had almost limitless food options and he chose poorly. In the same way, we have many spiritual options, but it is choosing the biblical food that provides healthy spiritual living.

Thought Questions

1. What evidence points to the Bible truly being the Word of God?
2. What was your first experience with the Bible?
3. In what ways has the Bible impacted your life?
4. How do you use the Bible in your life?
5. In what ways do you look to the Bible to identify parts of your life that need to change?

Chapter Two

Interpreting the Bible

Some think that interpretation of the Bible is completely subjective, and one can take whatever he or she wants from the teaching of the Bible. Everyone's personal interpretation is just as valid as anybody else's. But this is certainly not the way the prophets and apostles of old understood the Bible.

The seventh century BCE prophet Jeremiah warned the Israelites against teachers who were falsely claiming they were speaking oracles of God. An oracle was a message of God spoken through a human intermediary, typically a priest or prophet. Jeremiah wrote to the false teachers saying, "You must not mention 'the oracle of the LORD' again, because every man's own word becomes his oracle and so you distort the words of the living God, the LORD Almighty, our God" (Jer. 23:36). God was letting the people know that there is a difference between humankind's interpretation and God's instructions. Humankind's word is *not* God's Word. God was warning the people against *distorting* his Word. If it is possible to distort God's Word, then the interpretation of God's Word cannot be completely subjective. If interpretation were completely subjective, it would be impossible to distort God's Word because everyone's interpretation would be valid.

Paul angrily warned the Galatians that some were perverting the gospel in their teaching.

> I am astonished that you are so quickly deserting the one
> who called you by the grace of Christ and are turning

to a different gospel—which is really no gospel at all. Evidently some people are throwing you into confusion and are trying to pervert the gospel of Christ. (Gal.1:6–7)

If it is possible to pervert the gospel, then the interpretation of the gospel cannot be completely subjective. If interpretation were completely subjective, it would be impossible to pervert the gospel because everyone's interpretation would be valid.

Even our traditions, though typically conceived with good intent to help people live the godly life, can distort the teachings of God. Traditions are formed to help establish rules of good living and practice. But sometimes these human rules run afoul with God's teaching in scripture. For instance, the Jews had a tradition that honored a gift pledged to the temple treasury to encourage people to give to God. But some people were pledging money to the temple treasury that was deeply needed by their own family for basic needs. Jesus pointed out that caring for the basic needs of one's family was the higher priority. Jesus warned against traditions of humankind that stood contrary to biblical teaching and principles. "You nullify the word of God by your *tradition* that you have handed down" (Mk.7:13).

Most of the time Bible passages are easy to read and understand. You don't need to think too deeply about interpretation. But sometimes they aren't. Sometimes the passage appears vague and ambiguous. Sometimes people voice conflicting interpretations, and at first glance you're not sure whose perspective to accept. This is really when you need a set of rules or principles to help guide you through Bible study.

Just as it is clear biblical interpretation is not purely subjective, neither is it fully objective. In most cases we are examining evidence and making judgments of interpretation based on that evidence. Luckily, there are tools, or principles of interpretation, to help us avoid many of the purely subjective mistakes that are common in interpretation. When I reference objective Bible interpretation, it is in reference to using these types of principles that move us away from subjectivity and closer to objectivity.

The Importance of Hermeneutic Rules

There have been tremendous technological and perspective changes in the thousands of years since the original biblical documents were written. Earth's population has grown dramatically in the centuries since the Bible was written. We are now connected to one another all over the world in ways no biblical author could have foreseen. They could not travel around the globe in their day, nor did they even know what the physical earth looked like beyond their own domain. Most ancient people, like Jesus, didn't travel more than two hundred miles from their birthplace.

In contrast, today we are connected worldwide by the internet, television, and telephones. We drive hundreds of miles without a second thought. Many people of today travel far beyond their own country's borders. We have seen pictures of the entire planet from space and now know a great deal more about our universe, solar system, and galaxy. So how do we approach these ancient writings and apply them in today's vastly different world?

After a number of years serving as a full-time minister, I was invited by a group of ministers to participate in a private monthly Bible study. At the study, we would address an issue or some biblical principle and talk about how to approach the subject. We would share our approaches and knowledge of the relevant passages and historical context. Quite frankly, I don't remember anything specific about any of the passages that we studied or any conclusions that we reached. I don't even remember the topics we discussed. What I remember is the impact the study had on my approach to Bible study.

I came to see in these studies that the principles or rules one uses to interpret the Bible determine the interpretive conclusions one reaches in Bible study. Without a set of objective principles or rules, Bible study becomes highly subjective and is often simply a means to condone or condemn behavior we decided beforehand should be condoned or condemned. Rather, we want to be led and shaped by God, even if that means dramatic changes in our lifestyle.

So the question then arises, how do you interpret the Bible so that it is not simply a subjective confirmation of what you already believe? How do you sort out which of the conflicting interpretations voiced by others really reflect God's intent? Is there a way to avoid the danger of distorting or perverting the message of God?

There are really two steps to understanding and interpreting God's Word when confronted with challenging passages: (1) exegesis and (2) hermeneutics. The first step (exegesis) is to understand God's message as it was originally intended for its original audience. Scholars have developed a well-accepted process or set of rules to help us understand the original message as it was written to the original audience. That process is called exegesis, which comes from the Greek term, εξηγεισθαι (*exegeisthai*), meaning "to explain" or "to interpret." The second step (hermeneutics) helps us apply these ancient writings to our own modern world. This is called hermeneutics from the Greek term, έρμηνεύω (*hermeneuō*), meaning to "translate" or "interpret."

These two steps overlap to some degree. So I have combined them into one single list of interpretation principles. These are principles that most people understand to be valuable in objective interpretation of the Bible. Although this may at first glance appear to be a large list of principles to consider, over time and use, they will become as natural as any other routine action in life.

Interpretation Principles[16]

1. Presume the Bible is the Word of God. This respect and awe shapes how one approaches Bible study. The Bible is described as the inspired Word of God (2Ti.3:16). God has given us all we need to live the Christian life (Jn.20:30–31; 2 Pet.1:3; Jude 3). Treat the teaching of the Bible as coming from the creator of life. It is he who best understands life. Yet, the New Testament should not be read like a codified law book. Although certain divine principles can be described as "law," like the law of physics, we are not under a divine legal code (Rom.3:21–24, 28; 4:1–5; 5:1–2; 9:16, 31–32; 10:3–4; 11:6; Gal.2:15–16; 2:21; 3:25; 5:4; Eph.2:8; Phil.3:8–9).

---

[16] *Interpretation Principles.* There are other rules or principles one might use to interpret the Bible that are not listed here. However, some of those are very subjective in nature and do not help if one is trying to move toward a more objective approach to interpretation.

Rather, we are in a *relationship* with God. The Bible is God's Word to us. It is a window to God.

2. Pray sincerely. Any study of God's Word should begin with prayer. Sincerely seek God's guidance and allow him to guide you. This will help keep you honest and looking for God's direction in your interpretation of the passage.

3. Don't add to or subtract from the Word of God (Dt.4:2; Prov.30:6; Gal.1:6–9; 2 Jn.9–10; Rev.22:18–19). Although the passages listed above sometimes refer just to the individual book in which it is found, they espouse a general principle that is equally valid when applied to the sixty-six books as a complete unit. We accept the sixty-six books of the Bible as canon by faith in concert with God's people of the past. Although not combined into one bound volume until later, these are the documents accepted by early first-century Christians as inspired by God. They were not bound together into one volume in the first century because the codex (book) had not yet come into general use.[17] It wasn't until the fourth century CE that church leaders, worried about heresies, concluded it would be good to publish an exclusive list of the documents that make up scripture—called "canon."

"Adding to the Word of God" occurs when one requires others to accept his or her opinion as if it were the Word of God. This is like taping a new page into the Bible that lays out your personal opinion and trying to claim it is God's Word. This usually happens through inference.

Inferences are conclusions built on circumstantial evidence. There are stronger inferences (only one possible conclusion) and weaker inferences (several logical possibilities). When one requires others to accept weak inferences as divine truth, he or she is "adding to" the Word of God. Jeremiah condemned those who tried to add to the Word of God (Jer.23:33–40). Paul fought those who tried to add to the Word of God

---

[17] *Codex (book).* The codex was the early form of that which we are so familiar today that binds multiple documents into one book. The codex (book), binding multiple sheets of papyrus together in one volume, wasn't invented until the first century CE, and it took time for the codex to replace the use of individual scrolls. The codex wasn't widely used until the third century CE. Additionally, nobody even thought of trying to bind all of scripture into one volume in the first century. That was a new concept.

(Gal.1:6–9; 5:1–12). John warned against those who tried to add to the Word of God (2Jn.9).

Subtracting from the Word of God occurs when one neglects teachings in the Bible as if the teachings were not from God. This is like tearing pages out of the Bible. Either approach, adding to or subtracting from, is a subjective modification to the Word of God, which skews the message of the Bible.

4. Establish the text. Ask which text or version you should use. Scholars look at the texts in the original language and determine which underlying manuscripts should be used.[18] Most of us cannot read the original language, so we use translations. As mentioned earlier, English translations fall into a wide spectrum of types from literal, like an interlinear,[19] to a paraphrase. Your purpose for the study of the text will probably determine which type of translation you use.

5. Study the important terms as they were used in the days of the author. The ancient languages do not always exactly parallel ours today. For instance, there are four ancient Greek terms that can be translated "love," each with a slightly different meaning.[20] Our English language blends all four of the Greek terms into one English word: "love." English is not as precise as Greek when it comes to the term "love."

Some ancient terms like the Hebrew קדש (*qadosh*) and the Greek αγιος (*hagios*) have been commonly translated in our English Bibles as "holy." But "holy" misses the underlying meaning in the original languages of being "separated" or "different." A good dictionary of Bible terms will be helpful here.[21]

---

[18] Hebrew and Greek versions of the Bible typically include footnotes with original language variations found in different ancient manuscripts.

[19] *Interlinear.* An interlinear is a word-for-word translation that follows the order and style of the original biblical language. Interlinears have the original language on one line and the English translation, word-for-word, under the original language line. Ancient languages didn't typically follow our modern syntax (word order in a sentence), so the translation is awkward in modern English.

[20] *Love.* στοργη (*storge*) family love; φιλος (*philos*) friendship love; ερος (*eros*) romantic sexual love; and αγαπη (*agape*) commitment to the well-being of the recipient.

[21] W. E. Vine's *Vine's Complete Expository Dictionary of Old and New Testament Words* (Nashville: Thomas Nelson Publishers, 1996) or James Strong's *The New Strong's*

6. Establish the genre (the type of writing, i.e., historical narrative, letter, poetry, apocalyptic, etc.) You don't want to interpret a passage literally if it was meant to be taken figuratively. For instance, the book of Revelation expressly tells us parts of this document are symbolic (Rev.1:20; 4:5; 5:6; 11:8; 12:9; 17:9–12; 17:18). There are other portions of the Bible that are poetry (Prov.8) and still other sections of different genres. Not everything in the Bible is of a historical narrative genre. Proper interpretation begins with an acknowledgment of the proper genre.

7. Establish the context. Look at how the passage under investigation fits into the surrounding paragraphs of the text. If you ignore the context, you can take several unrelated statements and slap them together into one continuous misguided train of thought. For example, the following is taken as direct quotes from several different places in the Bible and slapped together out of context to form an outrageous command.

> He went away and hanged himself (Mt.27:5). Go and do likewise (Lk.10:37). What you are about to do, do quickly (Jn.13:27).[22]

Although the above is an absurd example, it is very easy to fall into the trap of taking a passage out of its original context and using it in some unrelated fashion simply to support some concept the user is trying to promote.

8. Try to establish any relevant historical data. Understanding the world into which the passage was written helps us understand the purpose and meaning of the passage. There may be references in the text itself to historical situations, settings, or even writings. Additionally, there may be ancient nonbiblical writings from the same time period that could help us interpret the biblical text. There are many interpretations of scriptures written by rabbis and early Christian leaders (church fathers) that could

---

Expanded Dictionary of Bible Words (Nashville: Thomas Nelson Publishers, 2001) are two helpful examples. If you read the original languages, the Hebrew and Greek lexicons are essential.

[22] *Context.* This example of bringing three unrelated passages together out of context has been used by many over time. It is probably impossible to know who first used these three passages to show the absurdity of slapping three unrelated passages together out of context.

help give us insight into how the original audience might have understood the message.

9. Look at parallel passages. Look at other biblical passages that address the same or similar subjects. A good concordance, a Bible dictionary, or resources like the *Thompson Chain-Reference Bible* can help. All these parallel passages should be considered to fully understand what God has revealed. It's like looking at the subject from different angles. This gives us a much fuller and more accurate view and understanding. A view of anything from just one angle can be deceptive and important facets of what is happening can be missed. A magician counts on an audience only seeing the act from one vantage point.

10. Favor the initial obvious reading of the text, unless there is strong reason not to. The initial obvious reading is what you first think of when you read the text. It is the presumptive proper reading. However, there could be a strong reason to adjust your understanding based on some historical context or a deeper study of the original Hebrew or Greek terms. Starting with the initial obvious reading first, and only after that looking to see if there is *strong* reason to modify it, helps guard against interpreting the text to conform to a personal agenda. Don't let yours or someone else's agenda shape your interpretation. Let God lead you.

11. Follow the commandments and exhortations of God (Dt.26:16; Jos.1:8; 1 Sam.15:22; Mt.7:21; Ac.5:29). When Jesus says, "Love your enemies and pray for those who persecute you," we know the basics of how to act. We might have questions about what loving our enemies looks like, or what type of prayer we should say for those persecuting us, but we know we have been asked by God to do something positive along these lines. We also know that love does not mean harming our enemies. We know that praying for those persecuting us does not mean praying for their demise. "Love" is doing something for the well-being of the recipient.[23] In most

---

[23] James Strong, *The New Strong's Expanded Dictionary of Bible Words* (Nashville: Thomas Nelson Publishers, 2001), 907, §26 αγαπη. "It was an exercise of the divine will in deliberate choice, made without assignable cause save that which lies in the nature of God himself ... Christian love, whether exercised toward the brethren, or toward men generally, is not an impulse from the feelings, it does not always run with the natural inclinations, nor does it spend itself only upon those for whom some affinity is discovered. Love seeks the welfare of all, and works no ill to any."

cases, there is no problem figuring out what God wants. The problem, if there is one, is in carrying out what we know to be the right thing to do.[24]

12. *Take note of the priority in scripture.* Not everything is of equal importance. At times there may be a conflict between two teachings. For example, David and his men eat the consecrated bread reserved for the priests (Lev.25:4–9) when they were famished (Mt.12:3–8). Physical needs tend to trump rituals. Jesus explained that caring for one's father and mother takes precedence over the tradition of dedicating certain physical assets to God (Mk.7:9–14). Family needs tend to trump the traditions of humankind. Paul spoke of an order of importance in doctrinal issues when he wrote that which is of first importance is the death, burial, and resurrection of Jesus according to scripture (1Co.15:3–8).

13. *Hold to the principle and not the practice if the practice is tied to the culture of the author.* Sometimes it isn't as clear as we would like. What happens to Jesus's command to "wash feet" (Jn.13) when foot washing is no longer a custom in our society? How do we follow Paul's encouragement to "greet one another with a holy kiss" (Ro.16) when kissing someone who is not your husband or wife may be offensive to the recipient in a particular culture? Some cultures use the kiss as a general greeting. Other cultures, like the United States, do not. I have a series of questions I ask myself to determine whether a teaching is meant for all people or whether it is tied to specific culture or set of circumstances.

a. *Does scripture itself expressly state the principle is for all?* This is rare in the Bible, but it does occur. For instance, in Acts 2, Peter gives us the first Christian sermon. When the people asked him what they should do, he answered and followed it with a promise that he indicated was for all people. "The promise is for you and your children and for all who are far off—for all whom the Lord our God will call" (Ac.2:39). If the Bible says the teaching is for all people, it probably is.

---

[24] *Love your enemies.* The question arises, what about police and military action? Is there no case for taking the life of another? Most believe that police and military action is part of the ordering of society with governments given the power to maintain order even including actions that sometimes take the life of dangerous wrongdoers (Ro.13:1–5). However, there are others who believe even police and the military should refrain from the taking of human life.

b. What is the strength and consistency of the teaching throughout the Bible? If the teaching is consistent through different time periods and settings, it probably is a teaching for all people of all times and circumstances. If the teaching on a particular topic is *not* consistent throughout the Bible, it is probably *not* meant for all people of all time. The inconsistency reveals that the teaching is time and situation specific. There may be a consistent underlying principle for all people of all time, but the practice itself varies from one situation to the next.

c. Did the author's pagan or secular culture permit alternatives? If the biblical teaching stands *against* the principles permitted in the author's pagan or secular culture, it is clear the biblical teaching is *not* tied to the culture of the author and more likely a teaching for all people of all cultures. For instance, the New Testament teaching on sexual purity throughout the Bible[25] stood in contrast to what was permitted in the first century Roman Empire when the New Testament was written. Thus, the New Testament teaching on sexual purity could not have grown out of the pagan culture of the day and should not be dismissed as such.

How Much of the Old Testament Is Important to the Christian?

There are a great many teachings in the Old Testament that are not followed by Christians today. Christians live under the New Testament (New Covenant) established by Jesus (Mt.26:28). How do we know which teachings to maintain of the Old Testament and which ones to ignore? Do the verbal pictures of God and examples of people in the Old Testament have any value to Christians?

1. Old Testament teachings that are also taught in the New Testament. At times, the Ten Commandments (minus the one to keep the Sabbath) are repeated in the New Testament in the form of lists (Mt.19:16–19; Ro.13:8–10). Other times, individual teachings of the Old Testament show up in the New Testament as standalone teachings. Here are some examples of where the Ten Commandments of the Old Testament are repeated in the New Testament.

---

[25] *Sexual Relationships.* (Mt.5:28; 19:4–6; Mk.7:22–23; 10:6–9; Ro.1:26–27; 1 Co.6:9–20; 2Co.12:21; Gal.5:19; Eph.5:13; 5:31; Col.3:15; 1 Tim.1:9–11; Heb.13:14; Jude 7)

Commandment	New Testament Parallel
1st Ex.20:3	Mt.4:10; 22:37–38; Lk.4:8; Rev.14:7
2nd Ex.20:4–6	Jn.4:24; Ac.15:20; 1Co.6:9–10; Gal.5:19–20; Eph.5:5
3rd Ex.20:7	Mt.5:19; 5:33-37; 1Ti.6:1; Ja.2:7
5th Ex.20:12	Mt.15:4–9; 19:19; Mk.10:19; Lk.18:20; Ro.1:29–30; Eph.6:1–3
6th Ex.20:13	Mt.5:21–22; 19:18; Mk.10:19; Lk.18:20; Ro.1:29–30; 13:9
7th Ex.20:14	Mt.5:27–28; 19:18; Mk.10:11–12, 19; Lk.16:18; 18:20; Ro.7:2–3; 13:9
8th Ex.20:15	Mt.19:18; Mk.10:19; Lk.18:20; Ro.13:9; Eph.4:28; 1Pe.4:15; Rev.9:21
9th Ex.20:16	Mt.19:18; Mk.10:19; Lk.18:20; Ac.5:3–4; Ro.13:9; Eph.4:25
10th Ex.20:17	Lk.12:15; Ro.1:29; 7:7; 13:9; 1Co.6:9–10; Gal.5:19–21; Eph.5:3–5

When a teaching is repeated in the New Testament as a teaching important for the people of the author's day, we don't need to worry about whether to follow the Old Testament teaching. The teaching has been given afresh in the New Testament. Since these teachings are repeated as relevant teaching in the New Testament, we can be sure they are relevant to Christians and should be followed just as any other teaching in the New Testament.

2. Some Old Testament laws are fulfilled (given new meaning) in Jesus. Many of the Old Testament images and symbols have a new Christian makeover. These concepts described in the Old Testament do not disappear in Christianity. Rather they take on new symbolism and significance. The Sabbath (Heb.4:1–13), the priesthood (Heb.4:14–5:10; 7–8), the tabernacle/temple (Heb.9:1–10), and animal sacrifices (Heb.9:11–10:18) are all fulfilled and given new meanings in Jesus. Whereas in the Old Testament the Sabbath rest was a day of physical rest one day a week, in Christianity it is God's ultimate rest (and peace) in which we share. Christ is the new eternal high priest, replacing the need for a human high priest. Our bodies are the new temple, or tabernacle, of God. Christ is the ultimate sacrifice that replaces all Old Testament animal sacrifices. Hebrews is the best book to see how these Old Testament rituals were fulfilled and took on new character in Jesus, but there are other references to the new meanings in Jesus throughout the New Testament.

3. The first-century church leaders wrote a letter answering the question of how much of the Old Testament law should be observed by Christians. Acts 15 describes a council meeting that took place in 49 CE. Paul and Barnabas were bringing Gentiles into the community of God's people, and some Jews thought the Gentiles needed to follow all the Old Testament laws to be Christians. Paul argued they did not. The council, which included the apostle Peter, the apostle Paul, and James, the brother of Jesus, discussed the issue, reached a conclusion, and then drafted a letter to be sent to all the churches. Part of the letter read:

> It seemed good to the Holy Spirit and to us not to burden you with anything beyond the following requirements: You are to abstain from food sacrificed to idols,[26] from blood,[27] from the meat of strangled animals[28] and from sexual immorality.[29] You will do well to avoid these things. (Ac.15:28–29)

The leaders of the apostolic church concluded that there were very few of the Old Testament laws that Christians needed to keep. They were to (1) stay away from activities that might suggest to others that they were worshipping idols, (2) they were to stay away from eating foods where the blood had not been drained from the animal because blood was the symbol of life, and (3) they were to stay away from sexual immorality as identified in the Old Testament.

With these three tests, most questions about how many of the Old Testament laws should be kept today are clearly answered. We can move forward with confidence we are living as God desires.

4. Pictures of God. Above and beyond the law addressed by the Acts 15 council, the Old Testament often contains verbal pictures of God. The Psalms in particular help us see God. They are like a window into heaven

---

[26] "Idols" (Lev.17:7).

[27] "Blood" (Lev.17:10).

[28] Strangled animals (Lev.17:13–14).

[29] Sexual Immorality (Ex.20:14; Lev.18–20).

and the presence of God. These Old Testament passages are helpful to Christians because they help us get to know and understand God's heart.

5. *Examples of people.* The Old Testament also provides us with pictures of people with bad and evil hearts and people with hearts of love and faith. Though King David was far from perfect, his writings show us a heart of faith.[30] Jeremiah's struggles and lamentations give us comfort when we are struggling ourselves. We learn and are encouraged by these examples from the past.

Not an End in Itself

Application of the exegetical and hermeneutical rules or principles will enrich any Bible study—even of passages that appear at first glance to be easy to understand. These rules force us to dig deeper, observe more closely, and step into the passage in ways we can often miss without them. But they become essential to Bible study where interpretational differences exist among Christians or when you are having trouble understanding the passage.

We must always remember that the words of the Bible are not an end in themselves. Some people have great knowledge of the Bible and have the amazing capacity to quote hundreds or even thousands of verses, yet they don't know God. We must always remember that this written Word of God is given to us primarily to help us know and connect to God. Jesus once told the religious leaders of his day, [39]"You diligently study the Scriptures because you think that by them you possess eternal life. These are the Scriptures that testify about me, [40]yet you refuse to come to me to have life" (Jn.5:39–40).

The Bible is a tool and a window to God. It helps us see God and see ourselves through God's eyes. It helps us directionally to take the next step. God has given us his Word, the Bible, as assistance in the process of maturing into the person God wants us to be. It is God speaking directly to us.

---

[30] *David's heart.* 1Sa.13:14; Ac.13:22.

Thought Questions

1. What process do you use to interpret and apply the Bible?
2. Is your process of interpretation more objective, subjective, or something else?
3. Is there value in following a process of interpretation that aims at being objective?
4. Why is it sometimes difficult to look at God's Word objectively, rather than to simply use it to confirm what you already believe?
5. How does proper interpretation of God's Word lead us closer to God?

CHAPTER THREE

Studying the Bible

Access to the Bible

There are many ways of getting access to the Bible. The Bible is printed with both the Old Testament and New Testament in our traditional Bibles in every major language on earth. Bibles are printed with specialized notes appealing to a particular interest like archaeology or apologetics.[31] The Special Interest Bible Appendix at the back of this book includes a description of some of these.

The Bible is printed in segments—like the book of Psalms alone, the New Testament alone, or the Gospel of John alone. It is printed on cards or booklets with collections of certain passages that apply to specific issues or topics. It is printed on flashcards with one verse per card for memorization purposes. Verses are printed on decorative signs, bumper stickers, pictures, pillows, and quilts and blankets that can be hung or placed in a home setting. They are printed on banners that can be hung on a church building. I have the entire written Bible downloaded on my cell phone.

The Bible is available in several translations on CD or audio download. Often these recordings have multiple voices for the various parts, sound effects, and background music. They often come with brief introductions to each book of the Bible. I also have an entire audio Bible on my cell phone.

---

[31] *Apologetics.* Study of the arguments used to defend the Bible and its message from attack.

Bible Movies

There are a number of movies available that depict events from the Bible. The Bible Movie Appendix to this book includes a description of several of these. Some are better and more accurate than others. All of them have some speculative element in that they must visually portray what may not be described in detail in the text itself. For instance, Acts 9 recounts Paul's journey toward Damascus when he is hit by a bright light, knocked down to the ground, and sees a vision of Jesus. The Bible does not explain whether Paul was walking, riding in a wagon, or riding a horse or donkey to get from Jerusalem to Damascus. A film producer would have to make a judgment call on that when recreating the scene.

The Bible on the Big Screen by J. Stephen Lang is a review of Bible movies through 2007.[32] Surely there will be many more made in the coming years. If you want to watch the Bible, you can do so. For some, this is an engaging tool for learning and motivation. We had a foreign exchange student from Japan live with us for about a year while she pursued a graduate degree. She had just become a Christian before coming to us and had virtually no knowledge of the Bible. I found the easiest way to help her learn was to show her the movies and then answer the host of questions that arose from each viewing. Subtitles were available on some of the movies, and that made it easier for our student to understand the dialogue in the film.

There are also numerous videos on particular biblical topics. These typically have a lead instructor or panel of scholars to help you understand the text. Some take you to the holy sites of the Middle East to help you visualize life in biblical times. These videos can use computer graphics to reconstruct the tabernacle, temple, Jerusalem, and almost anything else.

Settings for Study

You can take any of the above content (text, audio recording, or video) and study them in different settings.

1. Individual. First, you can study individually. You can read the Bible on your own in your own quiet place. If it's difficult to carve out a

---

[32] J. Stephen Lang, *The Bible on the Big Screen* (Grand Rapids: Baker Books, 2007).

huge chunk of time, you can read in small segments and then spend the day reflecting on what you've read. You can also listen or watch the Bible individually and be encouraged.

2. Small Group. You can study in small groups of approximately two to twelve people. Jesus taught one-on-one with the Pharisee Nicodemus (Jn.3) and the Samaritan woman at the well (Jn.4). He also spent considerable time with his twelve apostles (Jn.14–17). These are groups that are small enough that you can each share how the passage touches you, encourage one another on a personal basis, and ask questions to fill in the gaps of your own knowledge and understanding. Typically, these small groups work through the Bible by either studying a particular book or by studying a topic and looking at the various passages that are relevant to it.

Bible studies are always most helpful when they include discussion on practical application of the principles being taught. Some recommend holding to an end date for the study to avoid the feeling that one is trapped forever in the study. But my experience has been different. My wife and I taught a small group that met in homes midweek for decades. Over the years, the participants changed, the study moved to different homes, and the group varied in size from a few to thirty people, the topics changed, but the study continued on. In my experience, Jesus's model of working with twelve is about as large as a small group should be because anything larger tends to inhibit the intimacy and openness of the small group.

3. Large Group. One can study in large groups of people. Jesus taught large groups at the Sermon on the Mount (Mt.5–7) and the feeding of the five thousand (Mk.6:30–44). The strength of this kind of study is that someone who is gifted and has a superior knowledge of the Bible often leads it. This provides opportunity to delve into the facts, settings, and biblical principles in a deeper way. Often speakers are gifted in a way that can emotionally move the participants. These groups are usually filled with an energy that only a larger group can provide. You might view your Sunday morning service assembly, a church retreat, or a conference or seminar as this type of large group for study.

Each of these types of study fills a different need, and I am personally involved in all three. I study individually and with small and large groups, with the written word, audio recordings of Bible passages, and with Bible videos. The last several times I have taught small groups on Revelation,

I finished with a special meeting on a Friday or Saturday night where we all shared refreshments and just listened to an audio version of the entire book of Revelation. The event takes about two and a half hours with an intermission halfway through, but it is a real help to feel the flow of Revelation after studying it in segments. I've also led small groups through the Bible with movies where we showed either a large part of a film or the entire movie on a Saturday night once a month followed by a brief discussion. Each method has been rewarding in its own way.

Types of Study

In addition to the different ways we can access the Bible and the different settings for Bible study, there are different types of study within each setting. This has to do with the purpose of the study.

1. Devotional. Devotional study is the type of study where we are seeking to know God better and looking for God to guide us in life. By walking with him step-by-step, we can grow to know God better. It involves contemplating what a passage is saying and what God is asking you to do. Devotional study typically focuses on one verse or one passage of several sentences per day. It can also be structured as walking through a biblical book over a particular period of time. It might be working through a nonbiblical book about God's teachings. The key though is that devotional study is primarily looking to draw close to and know God better.

2. Research. Research is what I do when I am trying to learn about God's teaching on a particular topic. I may look at a topical concordance and search out all the passages that deal with that particular issue. I may read a topical Bible dictionary to see what I can learn about a subject. I may read a commentary that provides me with background information about the historical setting and the original terminology of a passage. Although I also find life's guidance in this type of study, my primary focus is to learn information about the passage or topic. I do this a great deal when preparing to teach others.

3. Implanting. In this third type of study, our goal is to simply get God's Word into our souls on a regular basis. We plan some course for daily engagement. That may be to read through the Bible in a year.[33] It may mean following a devotional plan with predesigned passages and topics laid out for a specific length of time. The object here is not necessarily to get new information or to find guidance for some specific issue. Rather, it is to feed on the Word of God on a daily basis as part of the process of implanting his Word in my soul.

I have read through, or listened through, the entire Bible many times. Most of the readings move quietly past me without too much of an overt impact. Typically, it is a quiet reinforcement of what I already know and a reminder of how I should live. But every so often (more than I would expect), I read or hear something that strikes me. I will think, *Wow, I didn't know that was there.* Or, *Oh that speaks to the questions I was just asking!* As much as I have read the Bible over the period of my Christian life, it still surprises me when I find something I hadn't noticed before.

Quite often study involves a combination of these types of study. While seeking to implant the Word of God in my soul, I am also looking to grow closer to God. Here is a chart to help visualize the various ways we can study the Bible and help implant God's revealed Word into our souls. I use all of these approaches to study God's Word.

Read the Bible	Listen to the Bible	Watch the Bible
Study Privately	Study in a Small Group	Study in a Large Group
Devotional	Research	Implanting

---

[33] *One Year Bible Studies.* There are number of studies that break the Bible down so that it can be read day by day and covered completely in a year, such as Alan Stringfellow's *Through the Bible in One Year* (New Kensington: Whitaker House Publishers, 2014) or the *One Year Chronological Bible* by Tyndale House Publishers. You can also study the New Testament over the period of one year.

Getting It to Stick

The more you work with and wrestle with a text, the better you get to know it, and the better your chance of being able to understand it and apply it to your own life.

1. Mark It Up. Different people have different approaches to using their Bibles. Some physically treat their Bibles with special care to avoid unnecessary wear or damage. It is a precious collection of God's teachings. These readers are careful to handle it with respect, awe, and protection. They guard against the bending of pages, handwritten notes, or anything else that would put marks on this sacred book of God.

I, on the other hand, view my Bible as a tool to be used. I underline, circle, and asterisk important terms in my Bible. I draw boxes around special passages. I write notes in the margins. Then, when my Bible is so well used that only I can read it and the binding is falling apart, I discard that Bible and start all over again with a new one. For me, the Bible is a tool that should be used in whatever way makes it most effective for the reader.

Although marking my Bible does help me quickly find special passages or terms, that is not my primary reason for marking it. My primary reason is to reinforce what I am reading, to make it stand out, to help me fix in my mind where that passage is, and to associate certain notes with the passage so that I can see those notes in my mind when I read the passage—even in a Bible where the notes are absent. I learn better by marking in my Bible.

There are numerous articles on the web and in instructional books about reading and learning where the reader is recommended to take notes, circle words, box sentences, or make notes in the margin of the text to better understand and remember the text. Some call this "active reading." Writing notes in your Bible engages you in the reading and helps the material to stick.

2. Study Word for Word. Taking the time and energy to look at each substantive word in a passage helps implant the message as a whole in our hearts. Look up each substantive word in a concordance, Bible dictionary, or other reference book and write out the definition.

3. Paraphrase. Rewrite the passage in your own words. Wrestling with the passage and writing it out will also help you understand and remember it.

4. Pray. Pray about the teaching, encouragement, or warning found in the passage. Make it personal and apply it to yourself.

Daily Reading

It is important that we expose ourselves to the Word of God on a frequent and regular basis. I remember hearing one person say, "You shouldn't read the morning paper until you've read the Bible." Whatever we read first tends to shape our attitude for the day.

God's Word is our daily spiritual food. I will never forget a story I read once in some Bible class materials that illustrates this.[34] The setting was a family home at about dinnertime. There was a mom, dad, young son, and slightly older daughter. Mom reminds the kids before dinner to do their daily Bible reading. The son decides it's kind of a bother to interrupt each day with a Bible reading. So he explains to his sister that he intends to read all of his daily readings for the next week in one sitting that night. Then he won't have to worry about it for another seven days.

Mom overhears what her son has just explained and asks her husband to follow her lead. She announces to the kids that they are ready to eat the dinners for the coming week and everyone should get to the table. The boy asks, "What do you mean "dinners for the week'?" Mom explains that she decided it would be easier if she cooked and they ate all the dinners for the next week that one night. Then they wouldn't have to stop the other six nights to cook or eat dinner.

The boy is confused and comments, "But I'll be really hungry if we don't get to eat dinner each night."

The sister realizes what is happening and explains, "Mom is trying to show us that just as we need food every day to remain strong, we also need God's Word every day to remain strong."

The son realizes his mistake and comes to understand that we don't feed on the Word of God just to get information in our heads, but rather to spiritually strengthen our souls, hearts, and minds and to establish relationship with God. That should be done daily to keep us strong.

---

[34] I regret that I do not know who wrote the story or in which publication I found it. I found this in church curriculum material published decades ago and did not record this information. But the story was good enough that I have never forgotten it.

Not Enough Time

As many people do, I too have felt that I just didn't have time for *daily* Bible study. I run at one hundred miles per hour and taking even fifteen minutes out of my day to read and meditate on the Bible seems like a lot to ask. I mean I barely have time to shower, get dressed, and eat breakfast before I head out to work in the morning. I work a secular job full time, so there isn't a lot of time at work to shut myself off from work and study the Bible. I often have meetings at night with various groups of people, and by the time I am done with my day, I am exhausted and just want to vegetate. When I do have time (like on a Saturday), I'm reading the Bible and other books to prepare for some lesson I am to present.

And yet I know how important it is to feed on God's Word *daily*. And so, when I can't find prolonged periods of time to focus completely on God's Word, I figure out a way to make it happen anyway—even if only small readings. I may read a passage of the Bible while I'm eating breakfast. I may listen to a downloaded version of the Bible while I drive to work. At bedtime, I may pick up the Bible sitting on the small table next to the bed that is divided by days to read through the New Testament in a year and read a section. There is a way to bring the Word of God into your life on a daily basis. It just takes a conscious effort to make it happen.

Read Other Materials Too

Although we all need the Bible in our lives on a daily basis as a healthy spiritual foundation, this does not mean we should refrain from reading anything else. In fact, you probably won't be able to share the good news of Jesus effectively if you don't have some familiarity with other perspectives—even if contrary to the Bible. The apostle Paul was a master at relaying the gospel message in familiar themes, terms, beliefs, and presuppositions unbelievers had in their lives. Paul was preaching new ideas. But he began his discussions from a point that was already accepted by his recipients. Only when he had his audience on board did he move on to the new ideas and principles that arose in Christianity.

When in Greece, Paul knew the pagans had an altar to an unknown god. He used that as a starting point in his sharing of Christ. He also quoted a pagan poet. Both of these would have opened the way for receptive hearts in those who were listening.

> People of Athens! I see that in every way you are very religious. For as I walked around and looked carefully at your objects of worship, I even found an altar with this inscription: TO AN UNKNOWN GOD. So you are ignorant of the very thing you worship—and this is what I am going to proclaim to you. The God who made the world and everything in it is the Lord of heaven and earth and does not live in temples built by human hands. And he is not served by human hands, as if he needed anything. Rather, he himself gives everyone life and breath and everything else. From one man he made all the nations, that they should inhabit the whole earth; and he marked out their appointed times in history and the boundaries of their lands. God did this so that they would seek him and perhaps reach out for him and find him, though he is not far from any one of us. 'For in him we live and move and have our being.' As some of your own poets have said, 'We are his offspring.'" (Ac.17:16–28)

As kingdom people charged with sharing the good news of Jesus Christ, it behooves us to have a knowledge of the world around us. History, psychology, science, anthropology, and even a familiarity with popular fiction can be helpful in this regard. It gives us a common starting point and an open door to the person with whom we would like to share the good news.

There is one warning to which we should all adhere, however—one thing that we must not forget to do. Any extra biblical material should be judged in light of the Bible, just as the Bereans did when hearing the preaching of Paul for the first time (Ac.17:11). The Bereans knew about Old Testament scripture. Paul's message was new and different. So they went back to the scriptures they knew to determine whether Paul's message was consistent with what they knew to be true from God's Word. We should do the same with any new ideas brought to our attention. Look at the teachings in both the Old and New Testaments of the Bible and determine whether or not the new teaching is consistent with scripture.

There are times when our own interpretation of scripture can block our ability to see straight. As such, we should examine our approach to scripture and take the steps necessary to ensure we are looking at it as objectively as possible and not through some unsupported presuppositions that erroneously affect our perspective. Step back from what you want the passage to say and examine it with the hermeneutical principles discussed earlier in chapter 2.

Love God's Word

The Bible is a collection of God's love letters to us. We cherish love letters, read them over and over, and take in each and every word. They help us draw closer to the person who wrote them. I met my wife while in graduate school in Texas, but then I had to return to California when I finished my coursework where I was working with a church. For a number of months, we had a long-distance relationship. During that time, we wrote to each other. I know for me, I would read and reread her words as we waited for the time at which we could be reunited physically. Her words were precious to me. So it is with God's words.

The human scribe of Psalm 119 viewed scripture as God's love letters. "I delight in your commands because I love them. I reach out for your commands, which I love, that I may meditate on your decrees" (Ps.119:47–48). "Your promises have been thoroughly tested, and your servant loves them" (Ps.119:140). "I obey your statutes, for I love them greatly" (Ps.119:167). When the God of all creation sends his love letters, they are indeed something to collected, held, and cherished.

Let us love the writings of the Bible. Not because they bring life by themselves, but rather because they are God's love letters to us and they point us to Jesus. Our prayers are our love letters back to God. The Bible is a window to God and helps us connect with the divine power as the ground prong of this spiritual plug.

Thought Questions

1. In what formats have you studied the Bible (reading, listening, watching, etc.)?
2. Which is your favorite format and why?
3. Which size study group do you enjoy most (individual, small group, large group, etc.)? Why?
4. What type of Bible study do you think is most helpful? Why?
5. What do you do to help remember God's Word or get it implanted in your soul?

Part Two

THE SECOND PRONG
DAILY (CONSTANT) PRAYER

Do not be anxious about anything, but in every situation, by prayer and petition, with thanksgiving, present your requests to God. (Phil.4:6)

CHAPTER FOUR

Talking with God

What Is Prayer?

At its simplest definition, prayer is communicating with God. The terms most commonly translated "prayer" arise out of the concept of "petition" or "request." But prayer is much more than just a petition. It is asking, praising, thanking, confessing, questioning, and sharing the day's challenges. It is an expression of gratefulness to the God who provides everything. In some cases, our actions do the talking for us. More than anything else, prayer is interaction with God. Charles Spurgeon wrote, "True prayer is neither a mere mental exercise nor a vocal performance. It is far deeper than that—it is spiritual transaction with the Creator of Heaven and Earth."[35]

Like any relationship, a relationship with God requires communication. Can you imagine trying to build a relationship with your spouse, friend, or coworkers without communicating back and forth? What we say to God makes up our side of building that relationship with him.

The second prong on the three-pronged plug to access the power of God is prayer. Failure to pray is a failure to avail ourselves of an important power source. It is failure to establish a *relationship* with God.

---

[35] http://www.crosswalk.com/faith/spiritual-life/inspiring-quotes/31-prayer-quotes-be-inspired-and-encouraged.html.

The Need for Prayer

It has been said that "there are no atheists in foxholes." The thought is that when we are faced with the severest of challenges, we will turn to God in the hope that he really does exist and that he will answer our prayers. Abraham Lincoln, who was not a particularly religious man when he first took office as president, was locked in a fierce civil war that would take more American lives than any other war before or after. He turned to God during those challenges and wrote, "I have been driven many times upon my knees by the overwhelming conviction that I had nowhere else to go. My own wisdom and that of all about me seemed insufficient for that day."[36]

The Bible declares that people will turn to God when they realize they have no one else upon whom they can depend. "You who answer prayer, to you all people will come" (Ps.65:2).

We all need to pray. God calls on us to share our anxieties and troubles with him because he loves us deeply (1Pet.5:7). Just like a parent who wants to help his or her child through any struggle, God wants to help us through life. God also wants *to hear* from us, much like a parent wants to hear from his or her children (Ps.102:17; Isa.30:19; 1Pet.3:12). It is disheartening when an adult child goes long periods of time without contacting his or her parents. Parents long for that communication and closeness. It is not necessarily the content that is important, but rather the bond that arises from the communication and contact.

Sometimes we find ourselves not certain of what to pray for. When someone is physically struggling at the end of his or her life, do we pray for healing or an easy and peaceful end? When people are in an abusive relationship, do we pray for healing of the relationship or a way out? When someone is caught up in deep sin and we are fearful that our help may be enabling rather than healing, do we pray that God will give us the ability to continue helping this person as before, or do we pray for the strength to let the person hit bottom in hope that he will wake up, see God, and change his life's direction? Even the greatest of those who pray have times when it just isn't clear how or what to pray for. But God helps us in this process.

---

[36] Abraham Lincoln. http://www.crosswalk.com/faith/spiritual-life/inspiring-quotes/31-prayer-quotes-be-inspired-and-encouraged.html.

In the same way, the Spirit helps us in our weakness. We do not know what we ought to pray for, but the Spirit himself intercedes for us through wordless groans. And he who searches our hearts knows the mind of the Spirit, because the Spirit intercedes for God's people in accordance with the will of God. (Ro.8:26–27)

As Max Lucado says, "Our prayers may be awkward. Our attempts may be feeble. But since the power of prayer is in the one who hears it and not in the one who says it, our prayers do make a difference."[37] Regardless of how inarticulate our prayers might seem, God hears, cares, and knows what we need and what we are asking.

Sometimes all we can do is bring the issue or the person for whom we are concerned to God, not fully knowing what he will do. There is a story of a time when Jesus was in Capernaum and teaching the people who had gathered to hear him speak. Some friends of a paralyzed man carried their friend to the house where Jesus was speaking, but it was so crowded they could not get in. They didn't know what Jesus would do, but they wanted to lay this man before the Messiah in hopes that he could help in some way. They didn't say a thing to Jesus, but the actions of the friends told Jesus all he needed to know. "Since they could not get him to Jesus because of the crowd, they made an opening in the roof above Jesus by digging through it and then lowered the mat the man was lying on" (Mk.2:4). Jesus saw the man being lowered before him, recognized the faith involved in such an action, forgave the man's sins, and healed him so he could walk. Sometimes all we can do is bring our problems, challenges, anxieties, and hopes and lay them out before God and ask him for help. God often responds in ways more wonderful than we had imagined.

God encourages all of us to engage in prayer (1Chron.16:11; Mt.7:7; Mt.26:41; Lk.18:1; Eph.6:18; 1 Th.5:17; Jas.5:13). We all need this connection with him, as it is an integral and necessary part of the Christian life. Martin Luther wrote, "To be a Christian without prayer is no more possible than to be alive without breathing."[38]

---

[37] http://www.crosswalk.com/faith/spiritual-life/inspiring-quotes/31-prayer-quotes-be-inspired-and-encouraged.html.

[38] http://www.crosswalk.com/faith/spiritual-life/inspiring-quotes/31-prayer-quotes-be-inspired-and-encouraged.html.

The Model Prayer

The disciples once asked Jesus, "How should we pray?" Jesus's response has become what is known as The Lord's Prayer.

This, then, is how you should pray:

> "Our Father in heaven,
> hallowed be your name,
> your kingdom come,
> your will be done
> on earth as it is in heaven.
> Give us today our daily bread.
> Forgive us our debts,
> as we also have forgiven our debtors.
> And lead us not into temptation,
> but deliver us from the evil one." (Mt.6:9–13)

This serves as a model for prayer. It is not the only prayer that can be prayed, but it demonstrates the nature of prayer and the elements we should include when we approach God. Jesus gives us five principles to incorporate in our prayer lives:

1. Honor and praise of God. "Hallowed be your name" is a phrase that gives honor to the recipient of the prayer. Honor is an important part of prayer.

2. Calling for submission to God's agenda. The words "your kingdom come, your will be done, on earth as it is in heaven" are calling for God's rule to play out in our lives here on earth. God's kingdom is not a physical kingdom. It is the *relationship* with the king (Lk.17:20–21). But God desires that his people live his life here on earth.

3. Petition for needs. "Give us today our daily bread." Bread was the food of sustenance in ancient times. You've heard of people living on "bread and water." Those symbolize the most basic of our nutritional needs, and the model prayer petitions God to provide them. In addition to basic nutrition, our basic needs may include a place to live, medical care, and safety.

4. Seek forgiveness. "Forgive our debts." We all need forgiveness. None of us are perfect, and we all fall short of God's glorious ideal for us (Rom.3:10; 3:23). So we petition God for his forgiveness. In so doing, we also recognize that we too need to be forgiving of other people (Mt.18:21–35).

5. *Petition for Deliverance.* "Lead us not into temptation." Requesting God's protection and deliverance from temptation and the evil one is important. We pray that God will help us be victorious over sin, either by avoiding its temptations or by the courage and strength that comes from God to overcome it.

A Consuming Thought or Emotion

There are times when we are so consumed by a particular need, thought, emotion, or action that our prayers become focused on that single issue. When our lead minister of a church in which I was an associate faced a debilitating problem, we as a church spent time together praying for his healing. We weren't thinking about the various elements of the model prayer. We were seeking God's help for a specific situation.

At other particular times in our lives, we might be filled with a sense of adoration and awe of God's goodness and power. I have felt this sense of adoration sitting on top of a Montana mountain looking over the peaks of other mountains, amazed at the magnificence of God's creation. I'm not thinking of the five elements of the model prayer. I'm lost in a sense of wonder.

Other times we might be overcome with thanksgiving and gratitude for the way God has blessed us or the way the church or some individuals have reached out to us in the name of Christ. Every time I think about the way the church reached out to me after the death of my first wife, I am overcome by a sense of thanksgiving for the outpouring of love I received.

Sometimes that single thought, emotion, or action becomes so strong that it takes over all others in prayer. King David committed adultery with Bathsheba, ordered her husband to the front of the battle to be killed, and then tried to conceal the entire affair. David kept up the righteous king appearance while living in sin. When the prophet Nathan confronted David and David realized the depth of his own sin, he fell on the floor, fasted for days, and expressed his sorrow in a prayer that focused solely on his repentance. You can feel the sorrow and remorse in these opening lines as he poured out his pain.

> Have mercy on me, O God, according to your unfailing love; according to your great compassion blot out my transgressions. Wash away all my iniquity and cleanse me from my sin. For I know my transgressions, and my sin is always before me. Against you, you only, have I sinned and done what is evil in your sight; so you are right in your verdict and justified when you judge. Surely I was sinful at birth, sinful from the time my mother conceived me. (Ps.51:1–5)

The rest of the prayer in Psalm 51 reveals a man consumed with the guilt from his sin and the need for repentance. David didn't go through any five-step process of prayer to ensure he included adoration and thanksgiving. This prayer focused on the issues that were burning deep inside of him at the time. He needed relief, and confessional prayer was the way of obtaining it.

During normal, uneventful times, we can pray with the calm and organizational elements of the model prayer. It is good to remember to praise God, to ask for his direction, and to ask for his forgiveness and protection. At other times, we are so consumed with some particular issue that we simply drop to our knees and call out with a loud voice, "God help me!" or "Lord, thank you so much!"

Posture of Prayer

When it comes to the act of praying, we typically see images of people kneeling, bowing their heads, or joining their hands together pointed to the heavens. There isn't a required posture for prayer. Our physical orientation should be determined by the nature of the prayer. We have biblical examples of prayer posture in the form of bowing (Gen.24:26; Ex.4:31; 12:27; 34:8), kneeling (1Ki.8:54; 2Chron.6:13; Ezr.9:5; Ps.95:6; Isa.45:23; Dan.6:10; Lk.22:41; Ac.7:60; 9:40; 20:36; 21:5; Eph.3:14), face down on the ground (Nu.20:6; Jos.5:14; 1Ki.18:42; 2Chron.20:18; Mt.26:39), and standing (1Ki.8:22; Mk.11:25; Lk.18:11).

Once at a midweek college devotional meeting, we tried praying in different postures. We prayed standing with our hands lifted high to God. We prayed sitting with our hands together and pointing to heaven. We prayed kneeling, and we even prayed prostrate on the ground. Each position felt like a different type of prayer. We might stand and lift our hands to God in praise. We might lie prostrate on the ground when we are deeply sorrowful of our sin and need repentance. There are no black and white rules here. The posture will flow naturally from the type of prayer you are praying.

Private Prayers

Some prayers are private (Mk.1:35; 6:46–47; Lk.5:15–16; 6:12; 22:41–42) and some are public (Mt.11:25; Lk.3:21; Jn.11:41; 17:1). Sometimes we need to get away by ourselves to pray. Crowds of people constantly followed Jesus, and there were times he needed to get away from those crowds to speak earnestly with his Father in heaven. One day, "very early in the morning, while it was still dark, Jesus got up, left the house and went off to a solitary place, where he prayed" (Mk.1:35). The pull of people in need can be overwhelming at times. It is those times when it is best to go off to a private place to talk with God. The Bible says Jesus "often withdrew to lonely places and prayed" (Lk.5:16).

I remember when I was in graduate school in Texas and working with poor junior high kids from struggling broken families. The kids had real needs, and they gradually grew to view me as a type of surrogate parent. One day it seemed as though every one of them had some catastrophic problem. I was getting calls all day long until I really just couldn't take it anymore. This was in the days prior to cell phones. So I hopped on my bike and rode down the street past the staff youth minister's house to a place I hadn't even identified yet. I had to get away, find a quiet spot, and just pray until the anxiety calmed down and I could start thinking straight again. I loved each one of those kids, but when they poured out all their problems, it became too great for me to handle by myself.

There was one time when Jesus went off by himself to pray because he had a major decision to make. He was going to choose twelve men to serve as his initial ministry team. Jesus spent all night praying (Lk.6:12). Upon working out the answer to whom he should choose, Jesus came down from the mountain and announced the twelve apostles.

At Jesus's most challenging moment, just before his arrest, trial, and crucifixion, he walked a stone's throw away from the disciples, knelt, and prayed intensely to God. Here, away from those whom he was mentoring, he could really open up to his divine Father about the upcoming horror he was destined to face (Lk.22:41–44).

As a leader in a church who is often asked to lead public prayer, I know how easy it is to worry more about how I will be received by those who hear me praying than about real communication with God and the shaping of the hearts of those who hear the prayer. Jesus said:

> And when you pray, do not be like the hypocrites, for they love to pray standing in the synagogues and on the street corners to be seen by others. Truly I tell you, they have received their reward in full. But when you pray, go into your room, close the door and pray to your Father, who is unseen. Then your Father, who sees what is done in secret, will reward you. And when you pray, do not keep on babbling like pagans, for they think they will be heard because of their many words. Do not be like them, for your Father knows what you need before you ask him. (Mt.6:5–8)

God is looking for real, sincere communication. Private prayer is a guard against using prayer as a form of selfish showmanship.

Public Prayers

Yet there are times where public prayer is appropriate. Jesus often prayed audibly in front of others. As he did so, he prayed not to impress his followers, but as one truly focused on the Father in heaven.

Other times Jesus prayed out loud in front of others to teach those who were listening. When Jesus arrived at the tomb of his friend Lazarus, who had died four days earlier, Jesus prayed aloud so that the people present could hear the prayer and then see the dramatic answer to it.

So they took away the stone. Then Jesus looked up and said, "Father, I thank you that you have heard me. I knew that you always hear me, but *I said this for the benefit of the people standing here*, that they may believe that you sent me." When he had said this, Jesus called in a loud voice, "Lazarus, come out!" The dead man came out, his hands and feet wrapped with strips of linen, and a cloth around his face. Jesus said to them, "Take off the grave clothes and let him go." (Jn.11:41–44)

On a smaller scale, Jesus also spent time praying with his disciples in between teaching them, particularly in his final hours prior to his arrest and execution (Jn.13–16; Jn.17). He prayed for himself (Jn.17:1–5), for his disciples (Jn.17:6–19), and for all believers (Jn.17:20–26). This wasn't a crowd of five thousand, but it was praying before a small group of followers who had become his family.

How Often

So how often should one pray? The author of Psalm 88 writes of praying in the morning (Ps.88:13). David writes of praying evening, morning, and noon (Ps.55:17). For many of us, it is important to have a set time each day to ensure that we do pray on a regular basis. I prefer the morning. Sometimes my wife gets into bed and says, "Let's pray together." I typically fall asleep at night so fast that it is virtually impossible for me to have meaningful prayer that late.

But prayer is not just something we engage in at scheduled times. We are to pray without ceasing (2Th.1:11; 2Ti.1:3). We are encouraged to pray continually (1Th.5:19). How does one pray "continually" or "without ceasing?" Surely there are times when you think about something else. When one is asleep, can one still pray?

Continual prayer does not mean that you are verbalizing to God in a constant thread of conversation throughout each minute of every day. To pray continually, one must have the ability to see God as always present. God is our constant companion, in every situation, at all times, whether good or bad. We pray, audibly or with our minds, throughout the day because God is with us always. He is right beside me in every situation—like a friend who is there when I need him.

The musical *Fiddler on the Roof*[39] portrays Tevye as the Jewish father of five daughters living in Russia in the early twentieth century at a time when Jews struggled because of their religion. Tevye is frequently shown talking with God as part of his daily conversational life. He calls on God, complains to him, and questions the Almighty. The beauty of this portrayal is how naturally and easy Tevye has these conversations with God. Throughout the day, he talks with the Lord because he recognizes that God is his constant companion.

Praying constantly and without ceasing is knowing that God is present always and sharing your life with him throughout the day. Praying becomes a central part of one's Christian life. Although you may begin by praying at set times to get into the habit, prayer life should never be limited to only those scheduled times. And it should never be used as something to fall back on only when trouble strikes. As Corrie ten Boom asked, "Is prayer your steering wheel or your spare tire?"[40]

Prayer helps make us aware of God's presence and draws us into closer relationship with him. Engaging in prayer brings God and his work into our lives as a priority (Col.4:2). Focusing on God and his design and plans in prayer helps us develop godly lives (Ro.12:2). Prayer brings peace that surpasses all understanding (Phil.4:6–7). This truly is a powerful prong on the plug to God's power that we do not want to miss.

---

[39] *Fiddler on the Roof* is "a musical with music by Jerry Bock, lyrics by Sheldon Harnick, and book by Joseph Stein, set in the Pale of Settlement of Imperial Russia in 1905. The original Broadway production of the show, which opened in 1964, had the first musical theatre run in history to surpass three thousand performances. *Fiddler* held the record for the longest-running Broadway musical for almost ten years until *Grease* surpassed its run. It remains Broadway's sixteenth longest-running show in history. The production was extraordinarily profitable and highly acclaimed. It won nine Tony Awards, including Best Musical, Score, Book, Direction, and Choreography. It spawned five Broadway revivals and a highly successful 1971 film adaptation, and the show has enjoyed enduring international popularity. It is also a very popular choice for school and community productions." https://en.wikipedia.org/wiki/Fiddler_on_the_Roof, 2017.

[40] http://www.crosswalk.com/faith/spiritual-life/inspiring-quotes/31-prayer-quotes-be-inspired-and-encouraged.html.

Thought Questions

1. What is prayer?
2. When do you find yourself uncertain of what to pray for?
3. Do you try to remember the elements of the Lord's Prayer when praying? Why or why not?
4. Can you think of a time when you were consumed by one or two issues in your prayer life?
5. What value do you get from public prayers?
6. What value do you get from private prayers?

CHAPTER FIVE

Listening to God

How to Listen to God

We so often think of prayer as speaking to God that we sometimes forget there is a listening aspect of prayer that is just as important. Moses was initially shocked and frightened to hear God's voice speaking to him.

> Now Moses was tending the flock of Jethro, his father-in-law, the priest of Midian, and he led the flock to the far side of the wilderness and came to Horeb, the mountain of God. There the angel of the LORD appeared to him in flames of fire from within a bush. Moses saw that though the bush was on fire it did not burn up. So Moses thought, "I will go over and see this strange sight—why the bush does not burn up." When the LORD saw that he had gone over to look, God called to him from within the bush, "Moses! Moses!" And Moses said, "Here I am." "Do not come any closer," God said. "Take off your sandals, for the place where you are standing is holy ground." Then he said, "I am the God of your father, the God of Abraham, the God of Isaac and the God of Jacob." At this, Moses hid his face, because he was afraid to look at God. (Ex.3:1–6)

Over time Moses grew into a regular pattern of talking with God and listening for God's voice. Moses was never confused about who was man and who was God. He knew when he was first called that he had imperfections, would probably fail, and wasn't on the same plane as God. "Moses said to the LORD, 'Pardon your servant, Lord. I have never been eloquent, neither in the past nor since you have spoken to your servant. I am slow of speech and tongue" (Ex.4:10). This was a type of one-on-one between a man who knew he had serious limitations and the God of the universe. These conversations, speaking to God and listening for his voice, became normal for Moses over time.

We typically think of God's voice as a deep, powerful voice. We imagine a voice that booms from the heavens, perhaps accompanied by other powerful sights and sounds that assault the senses. The people of Israel were confronted with this form of God and they found it frightening.

> On the morning of the third day there was thunder and lightning, with a thick cloud over the mountain, and a very loud trumpet blast. Everyone in the camp trembled. Then Moses led the people out of the camp to meet with God, and they stood at the foot of the mountain. Mount Sinai was covered with smoke, because the LORD descended on it in fire. The smoke billowed up from it like smoke from a furnace, and the whole mountain trembled violently. As the sound of the trumpet grew louder and louder, Moses spoke and the voice of God answered him. (Ex.19:16–19)

> When the people saw the thunder and lightning and heard the trumpet and saw the mountain in smoke, they trembled with fear. They stayed at a distance and said to Moses, "Speak to us yourself and we will listen. But do not have God speak to us or we will die." (Ex.20:18–19)

But sometimes God's voice comes in a very different form. Elijah was having a tough time and needed God's encouragement, comfort, and guidance. To prepare Elijah for his words, God told Elijah to step out of his cave and stand on the mountain. Elijah braced himself for that familiar booming voice of God.

Then a great and powerful wind tore the mountains apart and shattered the rocks before the LORD, but the LORD was not in the wind. After the wind there was an earthquake, but the LORD was not in the earthquake. After the earthquake came a fire, but the LORD was not in the fire. And after the fire came a gentle whisper. When Elijah heard it, he pulled his cloak over his face and went out and stood at the mouth of the cave. Then a voice said to him, "What are you doing here, Elijah?" (1Ki.19:11–13)

We too need to listen for God's voice, which can come in many ways.

A Quiet Place

One of the best places to start one's practice of prayer is in quietness. Mother Teresa once wrote, "God speaks in the silence of the heart. Listening is the beginning of prayer."[41] The noise of life can often drown out God's voice. It is not that God is too quiet. It is that we focus on the external noises of life around us. We are faced with the noise of the TV, radio, clients, children, spouses, traffic, and a host of other sounds that demand our attention. I live in Silicon Valley, where the pace of life is hectic at best. There is so much going on. There is so much to distract us from hearing God's voice.

Audible noise isn't the only distraction. Even in the quiet rural areas of the world, there can be inner worries and concerns that shout louder than the voice of God. The concern about a child who is having problems, the dip of an economic crisis, or the shout of an angry neighbor or coworker can distract us from God. It takes concentration to hear what God is saying. God, through the psalmist, recommended, "Be still, and know that I am God" (Ps.46:10).

The voice of God may come in different forms, but it is imperative that we learn to listen. Getting off to a quiet place usually helps. You may find

---

[41] http://www.crosswalk.com/faith/spiritual-life/inspiring-quotes/31-prayer-quotes-be-inspired-and-encouraged.html.

it is a particular room or perhaps a closet in your house. Some people set up a prayer room. You may have a special place outside among the trees, on a mountain, or at the beach that brings a peaceful solace in which you can better hear God.

Some people use soft, soothing music; candles; or other aesthetic features to help create a mood for focusing on God. Others find these additions to be distractions. Each individual is different and what helps one person pray may distract another. You want to create your space in a manner that aids your ability to listen for God's voice. You may have to experiment a bit to determine what works best.

Although some can focus in on God regardless of what is happening around them, many of us need to grow into a practice of prayer to reach the point at which we can pray under any circumstance regardless of the noise around us. Eventually we should find that we are constantly connected to God by prayer, in every situation and every condition, regardless of outside noise. God's voice becomes our primary focus and everything else takes a back seat. For most of us, reaching this point takes time and maturity.

God Does Still Speak Today

The two most common ways we think of God speaking is through his written Word (the Bible) and through that quiet inner voice that lives within us. But there are other ways. Sometimes God speaks through a friend, acquaintance, or even someone we don't know at all. Oftentimes a mature Christian will gently guide another Christian through the challenges of life with great spiritual wisdom. But we have to be careful that our personal biases don't hinder us from hearing God's voice through the speaking of another.

I once attended an evangelism outreach event in Colonial Heights, Virginia. There were thousands of people present. One speaker came to the podium and began yelling at us. He yelled through his entire speech. It turned me off. In fact, it turned me off so much that I didn't listen to a thing he said. At the end, he called for people to make a new commitment to Christ. I stewed, thinking it was crazy to bring this guy here. Nobody is going to listen to him. Then about a hundred people went forward, moved by his words. I was astonished and thought, *What did he say?* I had not heard anything because of his style. The next time he spoke, I forced myself to listen, even though I did not like his style, and at the end of his talk, I also went forward to recommit my life to Christ. God was speaking through this presenter, but I didn't hear it the first time.

God might even speak through someone hostile for our well-being. As the Jewish religious leaders debated what to do with that troublemaker, Jesus, the high priest spoke up,

> "You know nothing at all! You do not realize that it is better for you that one man die for the people than that the whole nation perish." He did not say this on his own, but as high priest that year he prophesied that Jesus would die for the Jewish nation, and not only for that nation but also for the scattered children of God, to bring them together and make them one. (Jn.11:49–52)

Once I was at a special church event in Washington, DC. We had a well-known national speaker who had flown in for the weekend. At the evening program, the speaker began by praising the church. I listened without any objection as the speaker went through example after example of how this church was not falling into the traps other churches had fallen. Then part way into the sermon, an African American in a pullover white shirt with flowing sleeves stood up, faced the audience, and interrupted the guest speaker. He held up his hand and forcefully said, "Stop, stop, the Spirit is kicking me!" Like a prophet, he told us that rather than patting ourselves on the back, we should be out there on the streets reaching out to the people who need Christ. He admitted it was dangerous work, but we are called to reach out, not gloat in our greatness. Several members of the church tried to urge him to stop, but he kept talking. Finally, after perhaps five minutes, he was done, and he walked out of the church building. I didn't hear another thing the guest speaker said that night. I was thinking about what the impromptu man in the white shirt had said. I think God used that man to speak to us that night. He certainly spoke to me.

God also speaks in nonverbal ways through the beauty and intricacies of creation. How many times have you sat on a mountaintop, in a beautiful forest, or at the beach at sunrise or sunset and been moved and awed by the magnificence of the natural world? My wife and I have been going to Yosemite Valley every two to three years for decades. I look at the huge slices of rock and mountain covered by pine trees and waterfalls and dotted with wildlife of all kinds and can't help but think of the powerful imagination and care of God. This too is God speaking to us, and we need to stop and listen.

> The heavens declare the glory of God; the skies proclaim the work of his hands. Day after day they pour forth speech; night after night they reveal knowledge. They have no speech, they use no words; no sound is heard from them. Yet their voice goes out into all the earth, their words to the ends of the world. In the heavens God has pitched a tent for the sun. (Ps.19:1–4)

The Habit of Listening

Part of maturity in prayer is establishing a habit of listening as well as speaking to God. At first this may feel awkward. But eventually it will become a natural part of your prayer life.

Years ago, I heard the phrase "conversational prayer," and it helped me understand something new about prayer. Prayer doesn't have to be one continuous spewing out of words to God. It can be more like a conversation, where I say something to God and then listen for his response. I may then say something more and wait again for response. Conversational prayer can be used in groups where individual people share quick prayers to God in what might look like random order. Rather than one person running through a monologue with God, and unlike a specifically ordered prayer chain, conversation prayer looks more like our regular conversations. It's as if God were sitting there with us in the conversation—which he is in fact doing.

God speaks through his Spirit, which dwells within us and helps us hear and understand God's thoughts, attitudes, and directions (1Co.2:6–16). This may sound like a quiet voice inside our heads or hearts. E. M. Bounds wrote, "Prayer makes a godly man, and puts within him the mind of Christ, the mind of humility, of self-surrender, of service, of pity, and of prayer. If we really pray, we will become more like God, or else we will quit praying."[42] We need to listen to God's voice, however it comes.

Discernment

One might ask, how do I know if what I think I am hearing is really coming from God? What if I'm actually hearing the voice of Satan disguised as an angel of light? We are flawed human beings. We can be mistaken. What help is available for proper discernment?

I once read an article that explained help for discernment is parallel to the way the captain of a ship of the past knew when to turn in to the landing on a rocky coast.[43] Seafarers often placed several buoys in the water in a line to direct the captain. The captain moved slowly parallel to the coast until the buoys lined up. Once they lined up, the captain turned parallel to the buoys and floated safely into port.

Spiritual discernment works similarly. Our spiritual buoys are (1) the Bible, (2) that quiet inner voice, (3) circumstances, and (4) the words and encouragement from mature Christians whom you respect. When these four spiritual buoys line up, it's time to move with confidence in the direction indicated. Pray for wisdom in seeing the spiritual buoys and God will not fail you.[44]

A Warning and Promise

God is trying to lead and shape us. He calls us to himself to accomplish this. And so there is a warning to those who *will not* listen. God says, "I myself will call to account anyone who does not *listen* to my words that the prophet speaks in my name" (Dt.18:19). Additionally, God delivers a promise for those who *will* listen. "Blessed are those who *listen* to me, watching daily at my doors, waiting at my doorway. For those who find me find life and receive favor from the LORD" (Prov.8:34–35).

---

[42] http://www.crosswalk.com/faith/spiritual-life/inspiring-quotes/31-prayer-quotes-be-inspired-and-encouraged.html.

[43] *Ship story.* I don't remember specifically where I read this story, but I think it was an IVP booklet.

[44] *Pray for wisdom.* Ja.1:5.

It's tough to follow if you can't hear the call of the leader. Once we key in to his voice and come to know him, listening to God is natural for those who want to follow him. Jesus said, "My sheep listen to my voice; I know them, and they follow me" (Jn.10:27). The image of the sheep and shepherd is fitting. A baby lamb will follow the flock until he learns to recognize the voice of the shepherd. In like fashion, a new Christian often follows the example of other Christians until he learns to listen to and recognize the voice of God himself. Then that new Christian can become a leader, rather than just a follower.

In the Middle East even today, shepherds lead their sheep from one place to another. When they meet another shepherd on the road and stop to talk, the different flocks will intermingle. And when it's time for one shepherd to leave, he calls for his sheep and they separate from the other flock and follow because they know his voice.

Answering the Call

God calls all of us. We are called daily to small tasks of action and attitude. Each morning we should awake and listen for what God is calling us to do that day. We should continue to listen throughout the day. Keep in mind that the call could come at any time. It's not a question of whether he will call; it's only a question of when. The psalmist recognized this and wrote, "He *will* call on me, and I will answer him" (Ps.91:15).

Isaiah was a priest in the Temple of God. One day Isaiah heard God calling in a way he had never heard God speak before. Isaiah wrote, "Then I heard the voice of the Lord saying, "Whom shall I send? And who will go for us?" And I said, "Here am I. Send me!" (Isa.6:8). Isaiah heard the voice of God in the quietness of the temple and answered the call. How can we say, "Here am I, send me" if we don't listen for God's call?

Prayer is much more than just speaking to God. It is a two-way communication with God that involves thoughts from us to him and from him to us. Relationships that contain communication in one direction only are greatly hindered and will probably not last. Mother Teresa provided insight into her view of prayer when she shared, "Prayer is not asking.

Prayer is putting oneself in the hands of God, at His disposition, and listening to His voice in the depth of our hearts."[45]

Thought Questions

1. Do you think of prayer more as speaking to God or listening to God? Why?
2. How does listening to God draw you closer to God?
3. Where do you find it easiest to listen to God?
4. What was the most unusual time God spoke to you?
5. What can you do to avoid the noise that might drown God out?

---

[45] http://www.crosswalk.com/faith/spiritual-life/inspiring-quotes/31-prayer-quotes-be-inspired-and-encouraged.html.

CHAPTER SIX

Effective Prayer

Beth Moore noted, "There are parts of our calling, works of the Holy Spirit, and defeats of the darkness that will come no other way than through furious, fervent, faith-filled, unceasing prayer."[46] God has told us that we should confidently believe that he will answer our prayers (Isa.58:9; 65:35; Zec.13:9; Lk.11:9). Our faith is a belief and dependence on the fact that God has the power to do fantastic things far beyond our ability to even imagine. Jesus explained "Truly I tell you, if you have faith as small as a mustard seed, you can say to this mountain, 'Move from here to there,' and it will move. Nothing will be impossible for you" (Mt.17:20).

The Bible provides examples of amazing ways in which God has intervened in this world. The Hebrews saw the parting of the sea (Ex.14). They drank water that flowed from a rock (Ex.17). The next generation saw the defeat of Jericho (Jos.6). There was David's defeat of the giant, Goliath (1Sa.17). The dead were raised (1Ki.17; Jn.11), and people were healed of leprosy (2Ki.5; Mt.8).

I too have seen the power of God's intervention. I have witnessed people being healed through prayer. I have seen prayers answered in fundraisers receiving much more than I thought possible. I have prayed for people whom I thought would never turn to Christ—and then they did.

---

[46] http://www.crosswalk.com/faith/spiritual-life/inspiring-quotes/31-prayer-quotes-be-inspired-and-encouraged.html.

Praying Consistent with God's Desires

Prayer request must generally be consistent with the plans and desires of God. Is God going to grant a prayer request that he views as destructive or contrary to his plans and desires? Of course not.

Those who walk with God, follow his teaching, and dedicate themselves to his mission are much more likely to express prayer requests that are in line with God's will.

> I am the vine; you are the branches. If you remain in me and I in you, you will bear much fruit; apart from me you can do nothing. If you do not remain in me, you are like a branch that is thrown away and withers; such branches are picked up, thrown into the fire and burned. If you remain in me and my words remain in you, ask whatever you wish, and it will be done for you. This is to my Father's glory, that you bear much fruit, showing yourselves to be my disciples. (Jn.15:5–8)

The prayer of one who has faith, trust, and dependence on God is powerful because that person is living a life consistent with the desires of God. These people of faith want what God wants. More often than not, they pray for the desires of God. As a result, they pray with real power (Ja.5:16; Mt.21:22; Ja.5:15).

These are bold statements of the power of prayer when made by people of faith. In fact, God encourages us to ask. "Ask and it will be given to you; seek and you will find; knock and the door will be opened to you. For everyone who asks receives; the one who seeks finds; and to the one who knocks, the door will be opened" (Mt.7:7–8).

God wants us to turn to him and lets us know that we can do so with confidence (Eph.3:12; Heb.4:16). He is good and wants what is best for us. Jesus gives us several parables in which he describes the goodness of God in response to prayer (Lk.11:5–13; 18:1–8). God can be moved by prayer and grant requests because of his compassion for people.

Not Always as We Ask

Prayer is not always answered the way we hope or desire. Sometimes our prayers are not compatible with God's plan. There are at least two biblical examples of prayers by faithful people that were not answered the way the one praying had initially sought. The apostle Paul prayed three times that some "thorn in the flesh" would be taken from him, but God's answer was, "My grace is sufficient for you, for my power is made perfect in weakness" (2Co.12:9).

Paul went on to explain that he learned that it is Christ's power and not his own that is the real power. Paul was a man of great intellect who could annihilate his opposition in any debate. He had a dedication and perseverance matched by few, if any. So pride was always knocking at his door. We don't know what this thorn was, but God used it to teach Paul a very important lesson that led him to become one of the greatest Christian missionaries of all time.

Just before his arrest, Jesus spent a good part of the night in anguished prayer in the Garden of Gethsemane. He prayed, "Father, if you are willing, take this cup from me; yet not my will, but yours be done" (Lk.22:42). Jesus was asking that he be spared the torture, crucifixion, and death that awaited him. "Yet," he prayed, "not my will, but yours be done." Jesus was not relieved of the duty to face the cross. But his ultimate request that God's will be done was accomplished. It was this event that brought about forgiveness and the hope that people now have of spending eternity with God.

In both these cases, God had an overriding plan that he was going to accomplish. Where the prayers fit within that plan, they could be granted. Where they did not, God provided each with the answer that would best fit the needs of the people of God's family as a whole. It was best for Paul's own humility and effectiveness as a preacher to continue to face the thorn in his flesh and to rely on God's grace. It was best for Jesus to face torture and death on the cross to achieve forgiveness for the world.

I can think of only one case in the Bible where God granted an indirect prayer request that was contrary to his desire. But in so doing, he used the request and its consequence as a teaching tool. Additionally, he gave protective guidance to help lead the people within the setting they had requested. In 1 Samuel 8 the people of God asked the prophet Samuel for a king. They wanted to be led by a king like other nations. This displeased Samuel and he turned to the Lord. God responded to Samuel that their request was a rejection of God as their king. However, God told Samuel to listen to the people. He also wanted Samuel to warn the people about how human kings act. Samuel did warn the people, but the people continued to demand a king anyway. God instructed Samuel to give them a king. God had already foreseen this request being made and had given his people instructions on how a king of Israel was to conduct himself in Deuteronomy 17. Thus God reluctantly gave in to the request. But along with granting the request, he also provided guidance for a king and used their desire for a flawed human king as a teaching tool. The people of Israel quickly found out how flawed their kings could be.

Ineffective Prayer

Those who live apart from God and his ways are less likely to express prayers that are in concert with God's will. Thus disobedience (Dt.1:45; 1Sa.14:37; 28:6), indifference (Prov.1:28), a lack of mercy (Prov.21:13), a disrespect for God's teachings (Prov.28:9), cruelness (Isa.1:15), sin (Isa.59:2; Mic.3:4), stubbornness (Zec.7:13), wavering about God (Jas.1:6–7), and self-indulgence (Ja.4:3) are traits of someone who will probably not offer up prayers consistent with God's desires.

For instance, I might ask God to make me a winner of a $1.5 billion Powerball jackpot. I might ask God for a new Maserati, a mansion, or a job that pays a huge salary. I might ask God for my own fighter jet. My suspicion is that these are not the types of selfless prayers dedicated to God's service that will be granted. In fact, there has been a good amount of research that indicates getting every self-indulgent desire one wants is dangerously harmful.

This is not to say that a selfish person or one who has shown open hostility to God might not at some point call on God with a humble, repentant, and perhaps desperate heart. It is the true shape of one's heart that God looks at. And one who turns his or her life over to God will begin to change and become more and more like Christ over time. The penitent sinner's attitude will gradually grow to conform to that of God and his prayers will grow more in line with God's mission. That person's prayer life will become more effective as he or she matures in Christ.

Effective Prayer

Those who live for God and have committed themselves to his service are more likely to seek God's intervention in a form that matches God's desires and plans. Thus contrition and repentance (2Chron.7:14), committing wholeheartedly to God (Jer.29:13), belief and trust in God (Mk.11:24), aligning oneself with Christ and his teaching (Jn.15:7), committing to living God's life (Ja.5:16), and obedience to God's teachings (1Jn.3:22) are traits of someone who is more likely to pray consistently with God's desires and plans and see their prayers answered as requested.

God encourages us to seek his rule first. All else we need will eventually follow (Mt.6:33; Ps.27:4; 37:4–7). We just need to be patient. At the right time, God will provide. But it all begins with seeking him and his will first.

God is developing certain traits within his people—traits like humility, faith, hope, and love. Prayers aimed at the development of these traits are more likely to be answered in a positive fashion. For example, God promises to answer prayers from those who ask for wisdom in life (Ja.1:5). This is different from asking God to provide what I want. It is asking God to show me what *he* wants. It is asking for wisdom to be God's person.

What Prayer Is Not

Prayer is not a magical formula. It is not simply calling on the name of the Lord like calling on a genie in a bottle. We love the story of Aladdin, the boy who rubbed a magic lamp and a genie came out to grant him whatever he desired. Aladdin had only to command the genie and his wish would become reality.

But you can't call on Jesus like Aladdin could call on the genie. God is not to be commanded. Jesus once said, "Not everyone who says to me, 'Lord, Lord,' will enter the kingdom of heaven, but only the one who does the will of my Father who is in heaven" (Mt.7:21). The call of "Lord, Lord" must arise out of true faith, dependence, and commitment to God through Christ. It is not a formula, but rather a relationship.

Prayer is also not a guarantee against suffering. Jesus explains that we *will* face trials and persecution. Jesus warned, "I have told you these things, so that in me you may have peace. In this world you will have trouble. But take heart! I have overcome the world" (Jn.16:33). Jesus, God's own Son, faced horrible pain and death that fateful Friday after the Passover meal. The suffering was not avoided. Rather, what God did was to send an angel to minister to Jesus in the garden to strengthen and help him through this period of pain and tribulation (Lk.22:43). God had not forgotten Jesus and helped him make it through the most difficult time of his earthly life.

Great Biblical Prayers

One of the best ways to learn about prayer is to read the prayers recorded in the Bible. There are many. Some are short, and some are long. The book of Psalms is filled with some of the longer prayers. Some cover many topics and some only one. Some are characterized by praise and others by repentance. Some seek God's protection; some seek his guidance.

These are prayers prayed by people of faith over thousands of years. Those who pray are all human and thus are all flawed and fall short of the glory of God (Ro.3:10, 23). But these prayers of God's people help us understand the love and protection of God. They believed that God knew best and was worthy of their trust. These prayers are an intimate look at the spiritual hearts of those doing the praying.

As we begin our prayer life, we look to these great people of faith to understand how free and intimate prayer can be. We see their focus in prayer. We see the way they approach God with awe and respect. We see their concerns and the way they call on God. Sometimes they pray out of a selfish sense of vengeance. Yet even these misguided prayers are helpful to show what a flawed human being looks like in prayer and the expectation that God will hear the concerns of his people. Modeling is probably the best way to learn. Here God's people are modeling prayers for all who read or hear them. The Prayer Appendix at the back of this book provides a list of some of these biblical prayers.

The Power of Prayer

The Bible recounts a number of prayers that were answered by God's intervening power. Most of these are set in a particular historical situation from times long gone. As you read these prayers, imagine the parallel types of prayers you might pray in today's world.

Moses, who had walked and talked with God many times and had seen God's mighty deeds, once asked God, "Now show me your glory" (Ex.33:18). God agreed and revealed himself in a way Moses had never seen before. God led Moses to a cleft in the rock to partially hide him from the brilliance that he would momentarily see, and then God passed before him, covering Moses with his hand to protect him. It's almost like the precautions scientists take when viewing an atom or hydrogen bomb test. God is so brilliant that we can't look directly at him while in these human bodies. God gave Moses a unique ability to see God's glory as no one else had.

Somewhere between 1200 and 1050 BCE, Hannah, married to Elkanah, was barren and prayed to God for a child. This was at a time when childbearing was considered an important duty of a wife for the longevity of the family. Hannah "made a vow, saying, 'LORD Almighty, if you will only look on your servant's misery and remember me, and not forget your servant but give her a son, then I will give him to the LORD for all the days of his life, and no razor will ever be used on his head" (1Sa.1:11). The prayer was answered with the birth of Samuel. Hannah was true to her word and brought Samuel to the priest Eli when Samuel was a boy. Samuel became one of the great judges and prophets of the Bible.

Around the 850–800 BCE time period, a pagan king grew frustrated at the prophet Elisha's powers, which were hindering the king's plans. So he sent a large cohort of soldiers to surround and eliminate Elisha. At the sight of all the enemy soldiers closing in on them, Elisha's servant was deeply frightened. "'Don't be afraid,' the prophet answered. 'Those who are with us are more than those who are with them." And Elisha prayed, "Open his eyes, LORD, so that he may see" (2Ki.6:16–17). The servant's eyes were opened, and he was able to see the forces of God that were there to protect Elisha and his servant.

The Bible tells of the siege of Jerusalem by the Assyrian king Sennacharib at about 701 BCE. The king of Judah, Hezekiah, pleaded with the people to keep faith and pray for deliverance. Sennacharib sent a letter demanding surrender.

Hezekiah received the letter from the messengers and read it. Then he went up to the temple of the LORD and spread it out before the LORD. And Hezekiah prayed to the LORD: "LORD, the God of Israel, enthroned between the cherubim, you alone are God over all the kingdoms of the earth. You have made heaven and earth. Give ear, LORD, and hear; open your eyes, LORD, and see; listen to the words Sennacherib has sent to ridicule the living God. "It is true, LORD, that the Assyrian kings have laid waste these nations and their lands. They have thrown their gods into the fire and destroyed them, for they were not gods but only wood and stone, fashioned by human hands. Now, LORD our God, deliver us from his hand, so that all the kingdoms of the earth may know that you alone, LORD, are God." (2Ki.19:14–19)

A plague then hit the Assyrian forces, and they had to retreat back home to Nineveh to regroup.[47] Jerusalem was saved.

In 586 BCE, King Nebuchadnezzar of Babylon captured and destroyed the city of Jerusalem. He carried many of its inhabitants off to captivity in Babylon. During this captivity, King Nebuchadnezzar had a dream that none of his wise men could interpret. The king was so upset with his wise men that he threatened to execute them if they could not interpret the dream.

Then Daniel returned to his house and explained the matter to his friends Hananiah, Mishael and Azariah. He urged them to plead for mercy from the God of heaven concerning this mystery, so that he and his friends might not be executed with the rest of the wise men of Babylon. (Dan.2:17–18)

---

[47] *Assyrian Siege of Jerusalem.* The Assyrian records recount this siege and the return to Nineveh before the siege could be successful. The difference in the recounting between the Assyrian records and the Bible is that the Assyrian records explain the reason for the return as problems back home. The Bible describes the cause as a plague from God in answer to Hezekiah's prayer.

That night, Daniel was given the interpretation from God. He went to the king, explained the dream, and saved the people.

Jesus, as God incarnate, began his public ministry around 26 CE. Knowing that Jesus had the power of God, one Jewish man of local standing came to Jesus for help. In essence his request was a prayer to the God of the universe. The synagogue leader, Jairus, fell at Jesus's feet, pleading, "My little daughter is dying. Please come and put your hands on her so that she will be healed and live" (Mk.5:22–23). Jesus went to the place where the girl was lying and brought her to life again.

Following the death and resurrection of Jesus, Peter was imprisoned for his bold sharing of the message of Jesus Christ. While he was in prison, "the church was earnestly praying to God for him" (Ac.12:5). That night an angel appeared to Peter in the jail cell, his chains fell off, the gates were opened, and he walked out of jail with the angel without any hindrance from the guards. As they exited the jail, the angel disappeared. Peter immediately went to the place where the disciples were praying and shared his story.

Prayer is a powerful second prong of the plug that connects us to God. We share our thoughts and words with him. We align our prayers with God's mission. We receive his comfort and guidance in return. We listen for God's answer. We pray that our lives will be conformed to what God wants us to be. We pray that God will open our eyes to see the opportunities he has given us and to hear his call. It is this prayerful relationship with God that brings power.

Thought Questions

1. The biblical promises that God will answer prayer are bold. Why believe this?
2. How might you better ensure your prayers are consistent with God's will?
3. Describe a time when God answered your prayer better than you had imagined?
4. In what ways does living for God help make your prayer life more effective?
5. What great prayers have moved you?

Part Three

THE THIRD PRONG
REGULAR FELLOWSHIP
(PARTNERSHIP) WITH CHRISTIANS

Let us hold unswervingly to the hope we profess, for he who promised is faithful. And let us consider how we may spur one another on toward love and good deeds, not giving up meeting together, as some are in the habit of doing, but encouraging one another—and all the more as you see the Day approaching. (Heb.10:23–25)

CHAPTER SEVEN

Fellowship Is Partnership

The third prong on that three-pronged plug to the power of God is fellowship. We might also call it partnership. The Greek terms κοινωνεω (*koinoneo*—verb form) and κοινωνια (*koinonia*—noun form), commonly translated as "fellowship," carry the idea of sharing and participating in some venture with someone. It is having something in common and implies participation by all parties.[48]

A partnership is the joining of two or more people together for a common purpose. In the business world, it is a joint venture for profit. In Christian relations, the profit is not monetary. It is in building one another up, the growth of spiritual maturity of individual Christians, the strengthening of the church, and the spreading of the kingdom of God.

Upon committing to Christ, new Christians instantly enter into a partnership with other Christians all over the world. The Bible gives us a vivid picture of this community in the newly born church after the powerful infusion of God's Holy Spirit.

> They devoted themselves to the apostles' teaching and to fellowship, to the breaking of bread and to prayer. Everyone was filled with awe at the many wonders and signs performed by the apostles. All the believers were together and had everything in common. They sold

---

[48] *"Fellowship."* James Strong. *The New Strong's Expanded Dictionary of Bible Words* (Nashville: Thomas Nelson Publishers, 2001), §2814 κοινωνεω & §2842 κοινωνια, p.1191.

property and possessions to give to anyone who had need.
Every day they continued to meet together in the temple
courts. They broke bread in their homes and ate together
with glad and sincere hearts, praising God and enjoying
the favor of all the people. And the Lord added to their
number daily those who were being saved. (Ac.2:42–27)

It is one body and fellowship, connected by core beliefs and trust in
God, regardless of whether our ministries differ between individuals or
even church denominations. When the apostle Paul first met with the
early leaders of the Jerusalem church, there was concern over whether Paul
would be welcomed. He had begun preaching the good news to Gentiles,
and the earlier leaders had been preaching to the Jews (those circumcised
per the commands of the Old Testament). Would the leaders of Jerusalem
acknowledge the legitimacy of Paul's work? This issue was quickly resolved
when all agreed that they were part of the same fellowship and each had
a role in this amazing venture. Paul wrote about that meeting like this:

James, Cephas and John, those esteemed as pillars, gave
me and Barnabas the right hand of fellowship when they
recognized the grace given to me. They agreed that we
should go to the Gentiles, and they to the circumcised.[49]
All they asked was that we should continue to remember
the poor, the very thing I had been eager to do all along.
(Gal.2:9–10)

Partnership with the Divine

Christians experience this fellowship both on a tangible earthly level
and a divine one. Our partnership is solidified through God the Father,
Son, and Holy Spirit (1Co.1:9). The Bible even gives us a ritual,[50] or
practice, to remind us that we are in this partnership.

Communion[51] is a symbol of this fellowship. In communion, the

---

[49] *Circumcised.* The Jews.
[50] *Ritual.* An act that symbolizes something greater than the act itself.
[51] *Communion.* Also called "the Eucharist" or "the Lord's Supper."

unleavened bread and the cup of the Passover take on a special new significance. The Passover commemorated God's rescue of his people through the last of the ten plagues that befell Egypt in the days of Moses, some 1,200 to 1,500 years prior to Jesus and the birth of the church. In preparation for the coming of the last plague, the Hebrews were told to spread blood from a lamb over their doorposts, eat the lamb with family, and be ready to leave Egypt at any moment. They were to eat unleavened bread because there was no time to let the leaven rise. The angel of death would then "pass over" the houses of the Hebrews (Ex.12–13).

In that final Passover meal that Jesus shared with his disciples in the upper room, the elements were given new meaning. The bread was said to be Christ's body—both the body that was hung on the cross, and the church, which represents the body of Christ here and now on earth. The fruit of the vine represented his blood, shed on the cross for our sins. Jesus instructed his disciples to share this special meal as an ongoing remembrance. Communion is a ceremony of recognition that we are part of this partnership with Christ. Paul asks the rhetorical question,

> Is not the cup of thanksgiving for which we give thanks a *participation* in the blood of Christ? And is not the bread that we break a *participation* in the body of Christ? Because there is one loaf, we, who are many, are one body, for we all share the one loaf. (1Co.10:16–17)

Communion is an act by which we further proclaim our commitment to and partnership with Christ and with one another.

This partnership is a desire to know Christ. It is a willingness to share in his suffering. We want to be part of the team and undertake our participatory role in accomplishing God's purposes (Phil.3:10–11). This partnership is also with God's Holy Spirit. God's Spirit works within each Christian to guide and transform him or her into one of God's people (2Co.13:14). This partnership is a union with Christ and sharing with God's Spirit, united in purpose and venture.

> Therefore if you have any encouragement from being *united* with Christ, if any comfort from his love, if any

common *sharing* in the Spirit, if any tenderness and compassion, then make my joy complete by being like-minded, having the same love, being one in spirit and of one mind. (Phil.2:1–2)

Christianity truly is a partnership and participation with the divine and communion is a God-driven event to remember and proclaim this fact.

Partnership with Other Christians

The apostle Paul exhorts Christians to partner *spiritually* with other Christians and not unbelievers. It is counterproductive to join in partnership two people who have contrary understandings of purpose, commitment, and service. It would be like a business partnership where the partners disagreed on the direction of the company. These seldom end well. Paul wrote:

Do not be yoked together with unbelievers. For what do righteousness and wickedness have in common? Or what fellowship can light have with darkness? What harmony is there between Christ and Belial?[52] Or what does a believer have in common with an unbeliever? What agreement is there between the temple of God and idols? For we are the temple of the living God. (2Co.6:14–16)

As part of this spiritual partnership, we are connected to others throughout the world who are also committed to Christ. Although we come from many different cultures, those of us committed to Christ are all part of the same body of Christians. The apostle John explained how we are connected to one another through the Father and his Son, writing, "We proclaim to you what we have seen and heard, so that you also may have *fellowship* with us. And our *fellowship* is with the Father and with his Son, Jesus Christ" (1Jn.1:3).

---

[52] *Belial.* Found numerous times in the Old Testament (see Dt.13:13; Na.1:15). It was a Hebrew noun meaning "useless" or "worthless." Holman Bible Dictionary. Came to be applied to Satan or the devil.

It has always amazed me when I meet someone new and discover that person is a Christian, how we both sense an immediate bond that comes from our commitment to the same Lord. My first awareness of this came when I was in college and working at a movie theater. I was a projectionist, but one day I began talking with one young woman who worked the candy counter. We discovered we were both Christians. There was an exciting connection when we discovered we were both members of the family of Christ though we didn't go to the same church building and were of different denominations.

This experience has occurred many times throughout my life. In business we don't typically begin with a discussion about Christ, but sometimes someone mentions his or her church connection and the door is opened. Although I work in secular employment, my past work experiences in ministry are in my work profile, and my seminary degrees have hung on my office walls for years. People with whom I worked figured out I was a Christian and would come to talk with me about spiritual matters and sometimes to pray. It doesn't matter who is from what particular denomination. Partnership with Christ brings us into fellowship with one another.

Times have changed during my life as a Christian. It seems to me that when I first became a Christian, there was a great deal of denominational wall building. Each denomination was its own silo. Most knew very little about Christians in other denominations and often incorrectly labeled and profiled them. As contemporary Christian music began to develop and ecumenical events were planned, more and more young Christians from different churches were gathering together at the same concerts and events, and they brought back word to their own congregations that the others weren't really so bad. The walls began to fall.

Today, I am happy to say, there is a great deal of interaction and partnership between people of different denominations. Although each group may have its own way of approaching things, the overall commitment to Christ has caused many of those previous barriers to crumble. We are beginning to learn that what unites us is greater than what divides us.

Helping One Another

One of the ways this Christian partnership works is that Christians help one another to live the life to which God has called them. It is a team effort. The great Hall of Fame receiver Jerry Rice was brought to the San Francisco 49ers as a rookie in 1985. He had looked very promising in college and Coach Bill Walsh saw him as the new face of the team. But Rice had real problems for the first part of his rookie year. He dropped a lot of passes. Coach Walsh believed the problem was that Rice would try to start running for the goal before he secured the ball. Additionally, Walsh said Rice was hearing footsteps and focusing too much on the defenders who were ready to tackle him. Rice would turn his attention away from the ball to the defenders and the goal line before he had possession of the ball firmly in his hands.

Team members reached out trying to help Rice see his deficiencies and overcome them. Rice talked about how his teammates helped him during this tough time. "Freddie Solomon helped me a lot. My teammates kept their confidence in me."[53] Rice named other teammates who intervened to aid him through this crucial time. They all helped him understand that he needed to focus on the ball until he had full possession, and only then could he turn his attention to the defenders and where he wanted to run. Jerry Rice took his teammates' advice and became one of the greatest receivers of NFL history, helping his team win three Super Bowls.

Likewise, the church is a team of players who reach out and help one another. We don't just sit there and watch another player struggle. We get involved and try to help.

Mutual Protection

This partnership exists in part to assist Christians to avoid harmful situations. Christian brothers and sisters are here to guide one another. If you were at a party with a friend who was getting drunk, you wouldn't let that friend drive home alone, would you? Wouldn't you take his keys away? Even if he begged for his keys back, you would say, "No, I can't let

---

[53] *Jerry Rice.* "Football Outsiders." Michael Tanier. Nov.17, 2006. http://www. footballoutsiders.com/walkthrough/2006/too-deep-zone-jerry-rice-rookie-bust.

you drive." You would act this way not because you hated him or wanted to punish him, but because you cared for him and wanted to protect him from injury. Christians do the same with their Christian family members when they sense help is needed.

It is not judgmental to step in to help when you see someone who needs help. It is not putting oneself above another. We all need help because we all sin and fall short of God's ideal (Ro.3:10, 23.). We are all called upon to turn back to God when we lose our focus (2Ch.7:14; Eze.18:21, 31; Joel 2:12; Mt.3:2; Lk.13:2–3; Ac.2:38; 3:19; 8:22; 17:30).

Sin is devastatingly destructive. Upon seeing unrepentant sin in a brother or sister in Christ, out of love Christians should help lead a fellow Christian into repentance and back to God's lifestyle. Christians don't just sit by and watch. They get involved to help. Paul wrote, "Brothers and sisters, if someone is caught in a sin, you who live by the Spirit should restore that person gently" (Gal.6:1). This echoed Jesus's earlier words in Luke 17:3.

All of this is done out of love and concern for the well-being of the one who is falling short. Christians are to be there for one another like Jerry Rice's teammates were there for him. It is not judgmental to want to reach out and help. It is not placing oneself above another person. We all need help.

Learning from One Another

It is this type of team intervention that is part of the Christian partnership. When the apostle Paul was beginning his powerful mission work, he needed the help of others. When he first became a Christian, he was spiritually stuck until he received encouragement from Ananias (Ac.9:10–19).

Barnabas then reached out to Paul and started introducing him to others (Ac.9:26–27). Without Barnabas, Paul would have had a difficult time gaining acceptance in the church. Paul had been persecuting the Christians, and the community of faith wasn't sure they could trust him. It was Barnabas who helped open doors for Paul in the early stages of Paul's mission work.

Two of those people to whom Barnabas introduced Paul were Cephas (Peter) and James (Gal.1:18–19). These were probably the two most influential leaders in the church at the time. Paul references that he spent fifteen days with Cephas. We don't have the details of those fifteen days, but can you imagine the questions Paul might have asked as a newcomer to the faith or the stories Peter might have told? I can see Paul soaking up every word from this towering giant of faith.

Fourteen years later, Barnabas and Paul went to visit the apostles again in Jerusalem (Gal.2:1; Ac.9:27). This time Paul met not only Peter and James, but also the apostle John (Gal.2:9–10). Paul wrote he wanted to "be sure I was not running and had not been running my race in vain" (Gal.2:2). By this time Paul had been a Christian for some time. And yet, even at this point in time, he needed confirmation from Peter, John, and James that he was on the right track and not running in vain.

Paul was part of a team that included Ananias, Barnabas, James, Peter, and John. Paul made it clear that his calling came directly from God and not from any person (Gal.1:1, 17). But James, Peter, and John had been a part of the most pivotal events of human history. They had experiences he did not have. They had seen things he had not seen. They had walked with Jesus in the flesh. How could one not be in awe of James, Peter, and John?

Several years later, it was Paul who was helping Peter repent and be the Christian servant that he should be. Paul says:

> When Cephas came to Antioch, I opposed him to his face, because he stood condemned. For before certain men came from James, he used to eat with the Gentiles. But when they arrived, he began to draw back and separate himself from the Gentiles because he was afraid of those who belonged to the circumcision group. The other Jews joined him in his hypocrisy, so that by their hypocrisy even Barnabas was led astray. When I saw that they were not acting in line with the truth of the gospel, I said to Cephas in front of them all, "You are a Jew, yet you live like a Gentile and not like a Jew. How is it, then, that you force Gentiles to follow Jewish customs? (Gal.2:11–14)

The student had now become the teacher. In spite of this confrontation, Peter (2Pe.3:15) and Paul (Gal.2:8) continued to treat each other with respect and love.

This is part of the plan God has for his people. We don't sit on the sidelines and leave one's failings or victories to that person alone. No one stands or falls by oneself. We help one another. We intervene. We encourage. We share the wisdom we have gained in life with others. This is not done in a haughty, snubbing fashion, but rather in the tone of a caring teacher who wants to help another person succeed.

I doubt Paul would have grown into the dynamic missionary he had become had not Peter, James, John, and Barnabas interacted with and helped him understand what they knew. I wonder if Peter would have fallen into the hands of the Jewish legalists had it not been for Paul's intervention. I suspect Peter did not feel good at the moment he was being called out by Paul, but he didn't let that define their relationship. He had the maturity to realize that Paul was right, and he needed to repent.

This Christian fellowship and partnership is a powerful tool in God's arsenal of equipping us in our walk through life. We are much stronger together than we could ever be apart.

Thought Questions

1. In what ways do you see Christianity as a partnership (a) with other Christians and (b) with God?
2. In what ways should Christians help one another?
3. Can you describe a time when another Christian helped you get back on God's road to life?
4. When is Christian intervention harmful?
5. When is Christian intervention helpful and healing?

CHAPTER EIGHT

The Family of God

God's Family

Christian spiritual fellowship is with the people of God. We often think of them as the "family of God." A family is a group of people closely connected by marriage, birth, or adoption. The word is somewhat fluid in that, depending on the context, this could refer to the nuclear family of husband, wife, and children or the extended family including parents, grandparents, great-grandparents, uncles, aunts, cousins, and second and third cousins. The term can also be applied figuratively to many different associations of people.

In Old Testament times (about 2000 to 400 BCE), "family" translates two Hebrew terms, משפחה (*mishpachah*) and בית (*bayith*). The first could be applied to a wide range of people, including persons related by blood, marriage, slaveship, and sometimes even one's animals (as found in the fourth commandment, Ex. 20:10).[54] It might include the immediate family, tribe, or even nation. The second term had a much more restricted focus on those living within a house.

In the Old Testament patriarchal society, the oldest competent male held the highest authority in the family. He was the one legally responsible for every member of his household. But he was required to be a benevolent and loving father. The psalmist uses that societal expectation of a compassionate father to illustrate the compassion of God.

---

[54] *Family.* Holman Bible Dictionary in the software, WordSearch 11.

As a father has compassion on his children, so the LORD has compassion on those who fear him; for he knows how we are formed, he remembers that we are dust. (Psalm 103:13–14)

In the New Testament, Christian households appear to include one husband, one wife, children, relatives, slaves, servants, and possibly others. Their duties are briefly described in Ephesians 5:21–6:4 and Colossians 3:18–4:1, but a distinction was made between children and other members of a household.

God's Family

Each person who chooses to commit to God through Christ is a child of God through adoption. John notes that "to all who received him, to those who believed in his name, he gave the *right to become* children of God—children born not of natural descent, nor of human decision or a husband's will, but born of God" (Jn.1:12—–13).

This new birth is not a physical birth. It is a spiritual birth in which each one becomes a new person with a new spiritual family. We are spiritually adopted into God's family.

For he chose us in him before the creation of the world to be holy and blameless in his sight. In love he predestined us to be *adopted* as his sons through Jesus Christ, in accordance with his pleasure and will—to the praise of his glorious grace, which he has freely given us in the One he loves. (Eph.1:5)

Some mistakenly think that children can be born directly into God's family. At the beginning of the sixteenth century, just before start of the Reformation, it was common to think of the church and the state as one and the same. When one was born into the state, he or she was born into the church. When one was born into the church, he or she was born into the state. Baptismal certificates became certificates of state citizenship.

Some believe people are automatically Christians simply because they are born into a certain family, community, or nation. Some think they are Christian for life simply because of some ritual undertaken when an infant, child, or adult. Rather, the Christian life is a relationship with God and a continued commitment and allegiance to God and his leadership and empowerment.

Long before the Reformation, the apostle Paul clarified that one does not become a child of God simply by having been born into a particular heritage. Rather, it is those who walk in the faith of Abraham.

> It is not as though God's word had failed. For not all who are descended from Israel are Israel. Nor because they are his descendants are they all Abraham's children. On the contrary, "It is through Isaac that your offspring will be reckoned." In other words, it is not the natural children who are God's children, but it is the children of the promise who are regarded as Abraham's offspring. (Ro.9:6–8)

Jesus used examples of nuclear families to describe the nature of God's spiritual family (Matt. 7:9–10; 11:16-17; 21:28–32; Luke 11:7; 14:11–32). God's family displays the love, compassion, and kindness that a human family is supposed to exhibit. Just as we learn how a nuclear family should behave by the model of the church family, we learn about how the church family should function by the model of a loving, sacrificial nuclear family.

Closeness in the Family

Every family has its own set of house rules and expectations for its members. Most try to develop norms that build healthy families. The family members have to cooperate with one another to function as a unit. In most cases they willingly do this because of the closeness inherent in family bonds. Likewise, God has expectations for the behavior and attitudes of those who are adopted into his family.

> Therefore, brothers, we have an obligation—but it is not to the sinful nature, to live according to it. For if you live according to the sinful nature, you will die; but if by the Spirit you put to death the misdeeds of the body, you will

live, because those who are led by the Spirit of God are
sons of God. (Ro.8:12–14)

As Christians, we have been adopted into the family of God and are
now children of God with the promise of an inheritance of God's estate
just as a human child would also have a share in his father's estate. Paul
explains,

> For you did not receive a spirit that makes you a slave
> again to fear, but you received the Spirit of sonship. And
> by him we cry, *"Abba,* Father." The Spirit himself testifies
> with our spirit that we are God's children. Now if we are
> children, then we are heirs—heirs of God and coheirs
> with Christ, if indeed we share in his sufferings in order
> that we may also share in his glory. (Ro.8:15–17)

Abba is an Aramaic term of closeness that a small child would use
to describe or identify his father. Upon being adopted into the family of
God, we become children who grow ever closer to him in an intimacy
resembling that of a close loving family.

This adoption into the family of God brings freedom. It is freedom
from the bondage of sin, freedom to reach the heights of what we can
become only with God's help, and freedom to live with him in his eternal
home. We are granted that intimate closeness with God as our benevolent
father, just as a young child looks at his own benevolent parent. And
because of the nature of such a relationship, we are free to approach God
out of love and not fear.

> But when the time had fully come, God sent his Son, born
> of a woman, born under law, to redeem those under law,
> that we might receive the full rights of sons. Because you
> are sons, God sent the Spirit of his Son into our hearts, the
> Spirit who calls out, "Abba, Father." So you are no longer
> a slave, but a son; and since you are a son, God has made
> you also an heir. (Gal.4:4–7)

Becoming a child of God is the first step in becoming Christlike with the hope of truly seeing God.

> How great is the love the Father has lavished on us, that we should be called children of God! And that is what we are! The reason the world does not know us is that it did not know him. Dear friends, now we are children of God, and what we will be has not yet been made known. But we know that when he appears, we shall be like him, for we shall see him as he is. Everyone who has this hope in him purifies himself, just as he is pure. (1Jn.3:1–3)

Characteristics of the Family of God

It has often been said, "You can choose your friends, but you can't choose your family." That is also true with the family of God. We are brothers and sisters to every person who commits to God through Christ, whether we naturally feel comfortable with that person's personality and quirks or not. One perspective that helps me in this principle is the realization that we all have quirks of some kind. Some may never become our best friends because of our personality differences, but we still need to recognize they are our brothers and sisters in Christ.

David Horn lists several characteristics of Christian fellowship that really describe the family of God upon which our fellowship is based.[55]

1. Fellowship Is Nonexclusive. In the pouring out of the Holy Spirit in Acts chapter 2, we find that Peter addresses a group of people from many nations, customs, and languages. It can be both exciting and trying to partner with people from different cultures.

In Galatians 3:28, Paul tells us that Jews, Gentiles, slaves, free, male, and female all have the right to become children of God. Today people from every nation, every heritage, every race, and every gender are all invited to become part of the family of God and part of the Christian

---

[55] David Horn, *Soulmates* (Peabody: Hendrickson Publishers Marketing, LLC, 2017), 57–76. Horn goes into much more detail on each of these principles that is described herein.

fellowship. Although we are called to live according to a certain standard of holiness, differences do exist between us. And that's okay.

2. Fellowship Is Nonpreferential. No one is greater than another in the family of God due to wealth, secular power, looks, gifts, or talents. Believers are not to show favoritism to certain types of Christians over others (Ja.2:1). Paul explains that all of our gifts for Christian ministry are equally important in the sense that we need each of us to fulfill our calling and role in the Body of Christ (Ro.12).

3. Fellowship Is Nonreciprocal. We serve one another in fellowship without the expectation of getting something in return (Lk.6:35). We serve because (a) we love the other person and (b) service to that person builds him or her up in strength and maturity. We also serve and love others because God first loved us.

4. Fellowship Is Not Concerned with Status. We do not serve to gain personal status (1Co.12:25). Jesus warns against such thinking. Jesus pointed out that to be great in the kingdom of God, one must become a servant. He illustrated this point by washing the disciples' feet at the Last Supper, a duty normally left to a lowly servant (Jn.13). Jesus, the king of all, came not to be served, but to serve (Mk.10:45).

In today's world, with more people on the planet than ever before, we also seem to have a growing number who are lonely and lost. Many are lacking a strong family or group of friends. Humans are social creatures. We typically don't function well alone for long periods of time.

As members of the family of God, we are connected to a large and diverse group of people. Regardless of personality styles, educational levels or abilities, wealth, status, or anything else, if someone has committed to God through Christ, that person is a member of the family of God just as we are. And we need to treat them as such. That's what fellowship is.

Meeting with Those Outside the Family

Regular and steady interaction and relationships with Christians is an important factor in maturing into a strong Christian. This is one of the primary prongs of the plug to connect to the power of God. However, that does not mean we interact *only* with Christians and seclude ourselves from those who are not. We are not to be "rabbit hole Christians." Jon Johnson explains the problem.

> Many believers are "rabbit hole" Christians. In the morning they pop out of their safe Christian homes, hold their breath at work, scurry home to their families and then off to their Bible studies, and finally end the day praying for the unbelievers they safely avoided all day. (Jan Johnson, *Moody Monthly*, Nov. 1987)[56]

Interacting with unbelievers is important in a number of ways.

1. Opportunity. It creates the opportunity to share the good news of Jesus Christ, which we are charged with doing (Mt.28:19–20). How can we do this if we only interact with Christians? Paul raises this issue with a rhetorical question.

> How, then, can they call on the one they have not believed in? And how can they believe in the one of whom they have not heard? And how can they hear without someone preaching to them? And how can anyone preach unless they are sent? As it is written: "How beautiful are the feet of those who bring good news!" (Ro.10:14–15)

2. Learn. We can learn a great deal about life from unbelievers. There are some pretty smart unbelievers out there who can teach us about physics, history, anthropology, biology, psychology, great literature, and a host of other things. They may be able to show us something about relationships that we have missed. We don't want to deprive ourselves of this great learning because of our own fear of people who are different.

3. Maturity. Typically, we grow in maturity and skill as we interact with different kinds of people. We learn more about how people work. Sometimes I am compelled by employment, circumstances, or the call

---

[56] Jan Johnson, "Rabbit Hole Christians," from Moody Monthly, *Christianity Today* 32, no. 8, (Nov. 1987). https://www.preachingtoday.com/illustrations/1996/december/439.html.

of ministry to work with people who are very different from me. Those interactions may be extremely uncomfortable. Their dress, vocabulary, life perspective, or sense of entitlement may rub me the wrong way. But I have seen over and over again my patience in those situations helps me grow into a better and stronger person. I begin to understand how the other person thinks as I engage in personal interaction. I develop skills I wouldn't have without that interaction. These interactions help develop humility, compassion, and grace in my life. I can't understand someone with whom I don't interact.

Jesus's prayer in that last Passover meal confirms that we are not to separate ourselves from those who have a "worldly" or different perspective.

> My prayer is not that you take them out of the world but that you protect them from the evil one. They are not of the world, even as I am not of it. Sanctify them by the truth; your word is truth. As you sent me into the world, I have sent them into the world. (Jn.15:15–18)

We are not "*of* the world" in that we are pilgrims just passing through. Our real home is heaven with God. But we are *in* the world, here to help others and to lead others to the good news of Jesus Christ. We are placed on this earth to interact with people, regardless of whether they are believers or not. We just need to remember that our spiritual partnerships should be formed with those who are also committed to God through Christ. In other words, the people we commit to as a team to help build our connection with God and the fulfilment of his calling must be believers in the God of the Bible. Our spiritual partnerships are with Christians (2Co.6:14–16).

Lending Support

There are a number of ways in which Christians help one another as part of a spiritual family. I have been to the hospital many times when one of our members was facing serious physical challenges. The church mobilizes when someone is in trouble and reaches out to the struggling person and his or her family. I remember one time people from our church had pretty well filled the waiting room in response to a member's struggle for life. We were there to huddle around the biological family of the patient and lend whatever support we could.

There was another woman sitting all by herself unrelated to our church family who looked worried. Whereas we had come to lend support to our church member family, we also reached out to provide some support to this woman who was anxious about her child. It struck me how different it was that day. A number of members of our church had come to comfort the family of the patient we knew. This other woman would have had no one if we had not been there.

Reaching out to support and care does not only come from Christians. But God has designed his spiritual family to provide support and care to its members similar to the way a biological family supports its own members. When one is adopted into the family of God, he or she has a divinely made family of support.

Thought Questions

1. In what ways is the church like a family?
2. What expectations does your nuclear family have?
3. What expectations does God have of members of his spiritual family?
4. How do you interact with other Christians who are very different from you?
5. How do you interact with unbelievers who are very different from you?

CHAPTER NINE

The Church

Being in fellowship with God and Christians means I am part of a body that is here to encourage, guide, and assist other Christians in accomplishing the mission that God has given to each of us. This "body" is known as the "church." In the New Testament, the church is not the building. It is the people. Our fellowship is with those who are part of a local congregation and with all who are part of God's universal church.

There are a number of images given in the Bible to help us visualize the church. It is a spiritual building (1Co.12:27; Eph.2:21). It is a flock (Ac.20:28–29; 1Pe.5:2). It is the bride of Christ (2Co.11:2). It is the household of God (1Ti.3:15). And it is the Temple of God (1Co.3:16). It is useful to focus in on two additional descriptions to better understand the process of connecting to God.

The Church

The Greek term we translate as "church" is εκκλησια (*ekklesia*). "The word stresses a group of people called out for a special purpose."[57] We can see its general secular use in the Bible for municipal meetings (Ac.19:32, 39, 41). People were called out to meet together for some community purpose. Christians also used the term to describe their own assemblies as Christians (Mt.16:18; Ac.20:28; Eph.5:23; Col.1:18).

Most biblical references to the church are referencing a local

---

[57] *ekklesia*. James Strong, *The New Strong's Expanded Dictionary of Bible Words* (Nashville: Thomas Nelson Publishers, 2001), 1068, §1577.

congregation and not the universal church as a whole. It is clear from the use of *ekklesia* in the first century CE that this term included the concept of assembly. People were called out to assemble together for God's purpose. Some translations translate the term as "assembly" in passages like Romans 16:16 and 1 Corinthians 1:2. Christians assembled together, sometimes in small groups and sometimes in large groups, to undertake some work or purpose for God.

There's more to these meetings than just showing up, however. I met one woman who attended the general church assembly on Sunday mornings but then would run out of the church at the end of each service. She did not know the other members of the congregation, did not share meals with them, and had no partnership or participation with any of them outside of the formal Sunday morning church service. She was missing the purpose and benefit of Christians assembling together.

The idea of seeing oneself as part of the church and yet separate from all people (like some of the early monks) is foreign to the New Testament. In the New Testament, "church" is the gathering, fellowshipping, and partnering of Christians together for a common purpose. It is really difficult to fellowship or partner with other Christians when you have no contact with them.

The Body of Christ

The apostle Paul loved to describe the church as the "body" of Christ. He liked to use this description because it helps us understand how intertwined and dependent we are on one another. There is no "me" alone in Christianity. It is "we" as part of one whole body.

> Just as a body, though one, has many parts, but all its many parts form one body, so it is with Christ. For we were all baptized by one Spirit so as to form one body—whether Jews or Gentiles, slave or free—and we were all given the one Spirit to drink. Even so the body is not made up of one part but of many. (1Co.12:12–14; see also Ro.12:4–8; 1Co.12:27–31)

In both Romans 12 and 1 Corinthians 12, Paul gives examples of the types of gifts God bestows. These are gifts to enhance one's service for God. In the above passages, Paul is not trying to identify an exclusive list of the gifts given by God. Rather, he is trying to show us that there are many different gifts and yet we all work together for a common purpose. We all have different ways of serving as part of one unified body. No part is unimportant (1Co.12:15–30). We are all empowered by the same Spirit and for the common good (1Co.12:7, 11).

Not long ago I tore my rotator cuff[58] at my left shoulder after taking a fall. Most of the time surgeons can repair this damage, but not always. If not, the rest of one's muscles need to make up for what is lost. That is not always easy. So even though the rotator cuff appears to be a small, rather insignificant part of the body, those who live with unrepaired rotator cuffs know the loss of easy movement that accompanies that damaged part. Likewise, each Christian has one or more gifts to use for the body of Christ. When that gift is missing, the body just does not function as well.

Meeting the Needs of One Another

Christians meet together in part to discover one another's needs and to identify the resources that can help. Oftentimes it is the one who has been through a parallel struggle who can reach out and comfort the one who is presently engaged in the struggle (2Co.1:4). We tend to listen more attentively to one who has already been through it before.

Once we understand the needs of the people, we can better muster our resources to help those who need it. How can you possibly know the needs of your brother or sister in Christ if you don't *know* your brother or sister in Christ? You may be the only one who can say the right thing, provide the right help, or empathize fully with the person who has a particular need. But you won't be able to help if you don't know anything about that person.

In every church in which I have served, we shared information, as

---

[58] *Rotator cuff.* "The rotator cuff is a group of muscles and tendons that surround the shoulder joint, keeping the head of your upper arm bone firmly within the shallow socket of the shoulder." Mayo Clinic. https://www.mayoclinic.org/diseases-conditions/rotator-cuff-injury/symptoms-causes/syc-20350225.

permitted by the struggling person, with one another about the needs in our church community. We reached out to those in need. Sometimes we reached out privately and sometimes publicly to the church as a whole, depending on the need and the situation. In fact, a good portion of my present church's annual expenditures have been dedicated to people's financial needs. We usually know about the needs of the people before a request is made for help. This wouldn't happen if we didn't know the people.

Encourage Unbelievers to Commit to Christ

One result of our service to one another and our shared worship experiences is that others who are not yet Christians see the beauty and purpose of a Christian life and commit their own lives to Christ in response. The first church that met together and shared with one another grew daily in numbers (Ac.2:47). Churches that do not engage in this type of service and worship are often known for their failures.

Statistically, most people become Christians because of interaction with friends and relatives. Very few are converted by a street corner preacher or by a happenstance reading of a Christian book or the Bible. Those who are not part of the church need to see Christians at work to be drawn to God. The words of the Bible have meaning when one person witnesses another and can see how the biblical principles are lived out in a real human life.

In college I was involved in a midweek Bible study and devotional. We would get together, sing, pray, and share some personal life lesson. The group began my freshman year with only a few college kids. Little by little over the next several years, the numbers grew.

I'll never forget one of the visitors who attended one of our meetings and announced to me and one or two others afterward that this group couldn't be real. It must have all been scripted. It was too amazing to be real. We invited him to come back. He came back again and again and again. He got to know us outside of the weekly meeting. He finally realized that this was the real thing. He had found something he never thought could possibly exist. He found Christ living in us.

This is not to say that we were extraordinary Christians with amazing talents or gifts. We were just a bunch of college kids with no seminary religious training who loved the Lord and wanted to share our excitement and devotion to God with others. That was enough to lead a number of people to Christ over the years.

Sunday Morning

Traditionally, Sunday morning has been the primary day and time when the church gathers together. Early on in Christian history, Christians decided that Sunday, as the anniversary of the resurrection of Jesus, would be the primary day for Christian assembly. As such, most Christians today meet weekly on that day.

There are other meeting times. Some meet on Saturday or Sunday evenings. Some meet during the middle of the week. Most of the time these are smaller groups than the primary Sunday morning meetings, but not always. In the earliest accounting of Christian gatherings, Luke describes Christians meeting daily.

> Every day they continued to meet together in the temple
> courts. They broke bread in their homes and ate together
> with glad and sincere hearts, praising God and enjoying
> the favor of all the people. (Ac.2:46–47)

Later there is a description of Christians meeting on the first day of the week. Luke wrote, "On the first day of the week we came together to break bread. Paul spoke to the people and, because he intended to leave the next day, kept on talking until midnight" (Ac.20:7).[59]

There are no biblical commands that instruct us to meet on only

---

[59] *First Day of the Week.* This may refer to Saturday evening. In the Jewish calendar, which is what the Acts author used, the first day of the week began Saturday night at sundown. The reference to Paul preaching until midnight makes better sense if they were meeting on Saturday evening than if they were meeting on Sunday morning. Nobody had Sunday morning off in the first century. The Roman Empire didn't recognize weekends as days off. "Did the Ancient Romans Recognized Weekends?" Vince Rockston. 8/18/2014. https://aquilaelba.info/did-romans-recognize-weekends/. The Romans recognized that the Jews would not work on the Sabbath (Saturday), but the Jews' practice on the Sabbath was an exception to the rule that laborers did not take off on weekends.

one particular day or any particular time. But one who only meets with a small group at nontraditional times may be missing the benefit and opportunities that are offered by the larger groups on Sundays.

The Perfect Church

Many hunt for the perfect church by a practice known as "church hopping." This is visiting church after church until you find the church that is right for you. In one sense, this is a good process to match the personality of the church to your own personality. You won't probably fit with every local congregation, so checking out the church before you commit is a good practice. However, church hopping can also be ineffective and deceptive.

I have only been involved in this practice at one stage of my life. At all other times circumstances led me to the church in which I was engaged. This one case was different. My wife and I had been married for just over a year. I had just taken a new job. We had moved from the State of Maryland, where I worked with a Washington, DC, TV station, and I took a new job with a sister station in Lynchburg, Virginia. We didn't have any connection with any church in this new place, so we started visiting different churches with which we might fit. We visited one church one Sunday morning, another a week later, and another a week after that, and so on. I don't remember how many churches we looked at, but there was always something that just didn't feel right. We just couldn't find the perfect church. And so over time, we gradually lost interest and stopped going—anywhere.

Then one horrible evening, my wife collapsed in the hallway of our apartment. I called the operator, who called the paramedics. They arrived and tried, without success, to revive her. After the coroner and rescue squad left, I found myself all alone in my apartment in the middle of the night. I called my parents, then her parents, and then a minister I had from college in Montana. After we hung up, that minister in Montana pulled out a church directory, looked up a church in Lynchburg, Virginia, and called the minister of that church in the middle of the night saying, "We have a brother in need!" That Lynchburg minister and a good portion of that church reached out to me with companionship, prayer, food, and direction. I soon found myself a part of this church family and knew I had found a church home.

The interesting thing about this Lynchburg church is that my wife and I had visited this same church during our church hopping days and decided it was not for us. It just didn't impress us when we visited one Sunday morning. It wasn't the perfect church we were looking for. I soon came to realize that although they had nothing that was overly impressive on the outside, their love and service had come to move me deeply. In the end, this *was* the perfect church for me.

It is hard to know a church until you are involved with that church. You can only tell so much by the type of building, the quality of the music, or even the dynamics of the preaching. It is when you partner with the church in ministry that you really get to know the people and can learn about the nature of the church.

Engage in Ministry

Each of us should approach church with the desire to find a place to serve. I have been teaching Bible classes for decades. So I would probably seek out some type of teaching ministry at a new church. However, if that was not open, I might decide to sing on the praise team or choir on Sunday mornings, or help with benevolence to the less fortunate. Maybe I could help greet newcomers, visit the shut-ins, or engage with others in regular times of prayer. At the very least, I could reach out to people who are struggling, unhappy, or depressed.

I have been a member of five different churches over my Christian lifetime. I have always been able to find a place in each of these churches where I could undertake and engage in meaningful ministry. I simply get involved. I'm there when something is happening. I say yes when I am asked to participate, even if I have never undertaken that type of ministry activity before. As such, I have served in a host of different types of roles over the years. Some of these roles are up front and visible to the congregation, and some are not. I have carried out some roles better than others. The key is a willingness to engage and get involved with ministry. Opportunities will follow.

It is easy to be left out or forgotten if you simply wait for others to reach out to you. There is a lot going on in each of our busy lives, and it is all too frequent that we miss someone in need because of this. Chances are you will never be left out if you take the initiative. Ask where you can serve. Share your ideas. Pray for opportunities. Be respectful of others who don't share your dreams or concerns. Get involved even if it means doing something less desirable than your first choice.

Engaging in ministry helps me to hone my skills, learn about the workings of the church, and grow closer to other people. There is nothing that will help you grow close to others like working with them on some ministry activity for the purpose of serving others. There is no better way to learn about how the church works and can work than by becoming a part of that work.

Friends

People come in all different shapes and sizes emotionally. We have differing degrees of needs for closeness in friendship relationships. I married again several years after the passing of my first wife. My second wife, Sharon, and I have different needs when it comes to friendship relationships with other people. She and I talk about being best friends and we have a great time when we are together. But in addition to my time with Sharon, I am working full time in a secular job, spend a considerable amount of time in church service, and have hobbies that eat up time and put me into contact with others. Sharon doesn't have these to the degree that I do and needs something more than just me.

Sharon feels the need to be in a close relationship with other women. She needs to have one or more really close friends whom she can partner with in day-to-day activities like hiking, eating lunch, getting involved in some church activity, and just talking. She needs someone with a kindred spirit with whom she can share life. At times she has these friends close by. At other times they move away, and she feels the loss.

I don't feel that need as intensely as my wife. My life is filled with activity, and I don't even realize I'm missing a close friend. Unless someone raises the issue, I don't even think about it. I'm an extrovert, and I have plenty of people I call friends. These are people I know well and feel comfortable with in discussion or activities. In contrast to Sharon, I don't sense any need for that special close friendship beyond the closeness I have with Sharon and the friends I have from church and work.

So if you are like Sharon or others I know who need those close friendship relationships, then pray about your concerns and needs and get involved in activities where you can get to know people in a closer way than in a large general group of people. Be a friend to make a friend. Have patience with people like me who may not even think about the need for friends and may not be aware that you have that need. For people like me, the call is to be sensitive to others who do feel the need for that closeness in relationships and are struggling to find it.

Just Change It

Sometimes we are frustrated when our church doesn't address certain ministry needs or doesn't perform well when carrying them out. My suggestion is that rather than complaining or growing frustrated, we should seek ways to help change whatever isn't working well. There are many different ways to help affect change.

If I think something is needed, after prayer I can go to the existing leadership and share my concern or my plan. I can ask for assistance and guidance from the leadership. Sometimes all I am doing is lighting a fire in the hearts of the leadership to get some action started. Sometimes I may not know how to get something accomplished. I may simply see a need that is not being met. Sometimes it takes time to change things. So have patience. Hint: Don't frame the issue to church leadership as if it is the *failure* of the existing leadership. You don't want to start off by insulting and humiliating the leadership.

I typically believe that if someone has a passion for a particular ministry, there is a good chance God is calling that person to be involved in that ministry. He or she may or may not have the skills to plan or manage the ministry, but the passion is an important part of leadership. Most ministries fail without the driving passion of someone behind them. The person who sees the need and thinks it's important is someone who will work hard to make the ministry a success.

Encouragement

The bottom line for this third prong on our power plug is that we have fellowship with others so that we can encourage one another to be God's people.

> And let us consider how we may spur one another on toward love and good deeds, not giving up meeting together, as some are in the habit of doing, but encouraging one another—and all the more as you see the Day approaching. (Heb.10:24–25)

We meet together and interact with one another and participate in ministry activities together because it generates the encouragement that helps shape us into God's people. Our gifts are given for the common good of one another (1Co.12:7). We preach the Word of God to strengthen, encourage, and comfort others (1Co.14:3). Those gifts that edify the church are greater than those that only edify the individual (1Co.14:5). Paul continues, "Since you are eager for gifts of the Spirit, try to excel in those that build up the church" (1Co.14:12).

Our focus in meeting and interacting with other Christians is to build up, edify, strengthen, and comfort others. When we meet together with this attitude, it changes everything.

It has always fascinated me how two people can come to the same church service and one will be bored to death thinking he or she got nothing from the service, while the other will be lifted up and praising God. They are listening to the same message and singing the same songs. They are sitting in the same auditorium. What accounts for this difference?

Most commonly, the difference is in the attitude the two people have coming into the service.[60] If you come expecting to be entertained or deeply moved, you will feel let down unless the music is excellent and the

---

[60] *Difference.* It is true that a cultural difference in the way one church carries out its service can make someone from a different culture uncomfortable and distract the participant. The attitude can create differences even between people of the same culture.

speaker is profound. If you come to "get," you may not "get" what you came looking for and leave in disappointment. If you come expecting to be served but are not noticed by those around you, you leave frustrated that no one even stopped to say, "Welcome."

On the other hand, if you come expecting to reach out to those who are in need, you will leave feeling fulfilled. Just look around for someone who appears lonely or someone you know who is dealing with a tough challenge and reach out with encouraging words or prayer to that person. If you come to "give," you will be fulfilled because there are always ways you can give to those around you. If you come expecting to serve, then you will leave with a feeling of praise because you can always find a way to serve.

If you come expecting to give rather than get, it won't matter that nobody said, "Welcome." It won't matter that the music wasn't the best you've ever heard. It won't matter that the sermon was a repeat of teachings you have heard a hundred times before. You will still leave with a sense of fulfillment and praise because you were able to do what God has called you to do by edifying and building up the church.

Sitting on the Bench

There are times when we cannot give what we would as a healthy person. Divorce, death, depression, financial disaster, illness, abandonment, hostility, and a host of other challenges can beat us down. In sports there are times when an athlete may need to sit on the bench because of an injury. He or she needs time to heal before he or she can go back out on the field and engage in play. The athlete may never be able to play again as he or she could in the past. In like manner, in the church there are times when we are hurting or physically struggling to the degree that we can't function well and need to be fed and encouraged by others. But there are two important principles that we should remember about sitting on the bench.

First, a player only sits on the bench temporarily while he or she heals from injury. The bench is not meant as a permanent place of being. It is temporary.[61] Players who love the game long to get back into a role to help the team. That may mean recovering to the point of getting back to where one was before the injury. Or it may mean changing roles to one that is not as physically demanding. Players often move into coaching or commentator roles when they can no longer handle the physical nature of being on the field. For an active player who loved the game, sitting completely out of the game is rarely permanent.

Second, even when we are hurting, ill, injured, or simply cannot handle the physical nature of ministry as we had in the past, we can typically still be powerful in ministry. Even benched players encourage the active players. One elderly man from our church was confined to a wheelchair and had a host of physical ailments that limited his mobility. In this state he would regularly go to Starbucks in his wheelchair and meet with a group of people to talk about the Lord. When others were hurting, he was encouraging. His care for others during his own disability was a touching message of love to all who knew him.

I have seen this second principle of action a number of times. There was a woman I knew who had taught college in her younger days. The last time I saw her, she was dying of cancer. I went to see her in the hospital and brought my guitar to provide some comfort. When I left her room, I stepped into the elevator with two nurses. They saw my guitar and asked whom I was visiting. I explained, and they both immediately knew whom I had just seen. They shared with me and each other their amazement that she always sought to comfort and encourage the nurses who came in to care for her. She focused on their needs rather than her own. This woman continued to minister in spite of her illness and failing body.

There are times when we need to be ministered to. But typically these are temporary times. The death of a loved one, a financial crisis, a family challenge, a physical ailment or some other event may lead us to seek the encouragement of others for a time. But never forget to minister to the people God puts in front of you, regardless of your own hurt or limitations.

---

[61] *Temporary.* Only the injured or weakening player is addressed here. There can be other situations in which a player is benched for reasons of favoritism, retribution, or discrimination. That is a different subject altogether.

Sometimes ministering from those hurts or limitations can be a powerful message of hope for others.

Thought Questions

1. What do you think of when you hear the word "church?" Why?
2. In what ways is the church like a body?
3. Why is it important that Christians assemble together on a regular basis?
4. Have you ever church hopped? How did that work for you?
5. What do you gain by partnering with others and working with church ministries?

Part Four

THE CURRENT
THE HOLY SPIRIT

Then John gave this testimony: "I saw the Spirit come down from heaven as a dove and remain on him. And I myself did not know him, but the one who sent me to baptize with water told me, 'The man on whom you see the Spirit come down and remain is the one who will baptize with the Holy Spirit.' I have seen and I testify that this is God's Chosen One." (Jn.1:32–34)

CHAPTER TEN

The Holy Spirit of God

Holy Spirit Terms

Once you are plugged in to God with the three-pronged spiritual plug, the circuit is complete and the current can flow. The spiritual current that runs through the plug that connects us to God is the *Holy Spirit*.

"Holy" comes from the Hebrew term שרק (*qadosh*) and the Greek term ἅγιος (*hagios*), which typically function as adjectives. The foundational meaning of both terms is that a particular thing or animal is "set apart" in some way. In the Bible the terms are used for God as one "set apart from all else" or for God's people and things as "set apart for God's purpose."

"Spirit" comes from the Hebrew term רוח (*ruach*) and the Greek term πνευμα (*pneuma*). In general, these terms are used to refer to the "breath, wind, breeze, or spirit" of something. In the Bible they refer most commonly to "the mind, energy, and life of God." The Holy Spirit is the essence of God.

God's Spirit is mentioned in twenty-three books of the Old Testament and referenced eighty-eight times in those books. These references typically refer to "the Spirit of God" or some similar phrase. The description "Holy Spirit" is used only three times in the Old Testament.[62] The New Testament is filled with the phrase. The New Testament also uses other phrases to describe God's Holy Spirit. Robert Richardson wrote,

---

[62] *Holy Spirit in the Old Testament. Understanding the Holy Spirit Made Easy* (Peabody: Hendrickson Publishers, Inc., 2005), 6.

There is no subject more important in religion than that of the Holy Spirit. Unless this is properly understood, a large part of the Bible will remain unintelligible. On the other hand, a correct view about the Holy Spirit will do more than a knowledge of any other particular topic to give harmony, clearness, and consistency to what may be learned about all other matters presented in the Word of God.[63]

Divine Holy Spirit

The Holy Spirit, or Spirit of God, is described in the Bible as eternal (Heb.9:14), omniscient (1Cor.2:10f; Jn.14:26; 16:12f), omnipotent (Lk.1:35), and omnipresent (Ps.139:7–10). The Holy Spirit engages in creation (Gen.1:2; Job 33:4; Ps.104:30), regeneration (Jn.3:5), inspiration of the Scriptures (2 Pet.1:21), and the raising of the dead (Rom.8:11). This sounds a lot like God himself.

In fact, since the Spirit is the essence of God, all the attributes ascribed to God are also ascribed to the Holy Spirit. The Spirit is grouped with the Father and Son, who are deity (Mt.28:19; 1 Cor.12:4–6; 2 Cor.13:14). The works of the Spirit are the works of God (Isa.6:9f with Jn.12:39 & Acts 28:25–27; Ex.16:7 with Ps.95:8–11; Isa.63:9f with Heb.3:7–9). The Spirit is even called "God" (Acts 5:3f; 2 Cor.3:17f).

"Trinity" refers to the Father, Son, and Holy Spirit as three in one. The term is not used in the Bible, but the concept is. The Father, Son, and Spirit are all part of the Godhead and interchangeable in one sense. And yet they all have their particular role and distinct existence. The Father directs and initiates. The Son prays to the Father and is obedient to him. The Spirit replaces Jesus as a divine presence on earth. Instead of walking with people (as Jesus did), the Spirit lives *within* people (Ro.8:9 & 1Co.2).

You, however, are not in the realm of the flesh but are in the realm of the Spirit, if indeed the Spirit of God *lives in* you. And if anyone does not have the Spirit of Christ, they do not belong to Christ. But if *Christ is in* you, then even though your body is subject to death because of sin, the

---

[63] Ibid., 7.

Spirit gives life because of righteousness. And if the Spirit of him who raised Jesus from the dead is *living in* you, he who raised Christ from the dead will also give life to your mortal bodies because of his Spirit who *lives in* you. (Rom.8:9–11)

We are spiritual beings with God's Holy Spirit living *in* us. We are not just physical bodies. God's Spirit meshes with our souls to create something new—a body with Christ living in us. We are not purely objective beings who rely on factual observations, but rather souls who are being transformed from the inside out into a Christlikeness that comes only with God's changing power. We realize we are not to be simply intellectual in our approach. Our transformation means we are new creatures with new perspectives. This transformation occurs largely because of the work of the Holy Spirit, who lives within us.

A Person, Not a Thing

There is a tendency to view the Holy Spirit as a "thing." We may think of the Spirit as some force like that which is referenced in the popular Star Wars films. Or, as I have suggested in this book for limited purposes, we may think of the Holy Spirit like an electrical current. Part of this thinking comes from the fact that we can't typically see the Holy Spirit.[64]

However, the Bible describes the Spirit as a personal being with the use of personal pronouns (Jn.14:26; 26:13–14). Jesus spoke with his disciples earlier in the evening of the night he was arrested about the Holy Spirit coming to them. He spoke of the Holy Spirit using personal pronouns.

And I will ask the Father, and he will give you another advocate to help you and be with you forever—the Spirit of truth. The world cannot accept *him*, because it neither sees *him* nor knows *him*. But you know *him*, for *he* lives with you and will be in you. (Jn.14:16–17)

The Spirit is called the helper, comforter, or advocate, implying personal character (Jn.14:16, 26; 15:26; 16:7). Personal characteristics like

---

[64] *Physical appearing of the Holy Spirit.* There are at least two occasions on which the Holy Spirit could be seen in some visual form (Lk.3:22 & Ac.2:3).

intellect (1 Cor.2:11), sensibilities (Rom.8:27; 15:30), and will (1Co.12:11) are ascribed to him.

> For who knows a person's thoughts except their own spirit within them? In the same way no one knows the thoughts of God except the Spirit of God. What we have received is not the spirit of the world, but the Spirit who is from God, so that we may understand what God has freely given us. (1Co.2:11–12)

The Holy Spirit performs acts that a personal being would carry out. He teaches (Lk.12:12; Jn.14:26; 1 Cor.2:13; 1 Jn.2:27). He bears witness (Jn.15:26; Rom.8:16; Gal.4:6; 1 Jn.3:24; 1 Jn.4:13; 5:6). He convicts one of sin (Jn.16:8–11). He guides (Jn.16:13). He glorifies (lifts up) Christ (Jn.16:14). He calls people into service (Acts 13:2). He speaks (Acts 13:2; Rev.2:7). He directs (Acts 16:6f). He intercedes (Rom.8:26). He searches out the hearts of people (1 Cor.2:10).

Additionally, the Holy Spirit is grouped with other personal beings like the Father and Son (Mt.28:19; 1 Cor.12:4–6; 2 Cor.13:14), and he is treated by others as a personal being. He is tested (Acts 5:9), lied to (Acts 5:3), grieved (Eph.4:30; Isa. 63:10), resisted (Acts 7:51), insulted (Heb.10:29), blasphemed (Mt.12:31–32), and distinguished from his own power (Acts 10:38; Rom.15:13; 1 Cor.2:4). These are not the types of descriptions one uses for an impersonal force.

These passages all make it clear that the Holy Spirit is not an "it" or a "thing," but rather a living being just as the Father and Jesus are living beings. James Montgomery Boice points out our view of the Holy Spirit can have practical implications.

> "If we think of the Holy Spirit as a mysterious power, our thoughts will be, 'How can I get more of the Holy Spirit?' If we think of the Holy Spirit as a person, we will ask, 'How can the Holy Spirit have more of me?'[65]

---

[65] James Montgomery Boice, *Foundations of the Christian Faith* (Downers Grove: IVP, 1986), 374–375.

The Holy Spirit Does Not Come by Purchase or Formula

In Acts 8, Simon the magician was doing his thing in Samaria when he ran into Philip, the evangelist. Philip was able to heal people of physical ailments and demons. Simon listened. He committed his life to Christ and was baptized. But as he watched the power of Philip, he mistakenly thought that power was just a greater version of his own. When Peter and John came and laid their hands on the believers to pass on the Holy Spirit's power, Simon offered to purchase this great power. Peter's response was unwavering. "May your money perish with you, because you thought you could buy the gift of God with money" (Ac.8:20).

There were some Jews who later tried to cast out demons by using the magical formula, "In the name of the Jesus whom Paul preaches, I command you to come out" (Ac.9:13). But simply using the correct words does not work. This is because the power comes to those with the right heart, not the right formula.

The Spirit of God comes by God's direction and in response to faith when we commit to a relationship with him. It doesn't cost anything—except one's life. For we are to lay our lives down, becoming subjects to Christ our king. What we get by doing this is an infusion of God's Holy Spirit. The price is high but the reward tremendous.

The Work of the Holy Spirit

What is the work of the Holy Spirit? Minister and author, James Montgomery Boice, writes:

> We sense almost instinctively that our question is nearly unanswerable. For the Holy Spirit is God, as he is, then all that the Father and Son do, the Holy Spirit also does.[66]

There are many questions about the Holy Spirit that will probably be unanswerable until we see God face-to-face. However, in that upper room on the final night before Jesus's arrest, he explained to his disciples *why* the Holy Spirit was coming to them. He called God's Holy Spirit

---

[66] Boice, *Foundations of the Christian Faith*, Ibid., 380.

"the Advocate." The Advocate was coming to testify about Jesus, whom they themselves would testifying about soon (Jn.15:26–27). Jesus told them it was good that he was going away so that the Advocate could come (Jn.16:7). Jesus was about to be crucified, resurrected, and then lifted up to heaven. He would be gone from this physical world and unavailable to his disciples. God's Spirit was to take the place of Jesus here on earth so that his disciples would not be left alone (Jn.16:7).

The term "advocate" translates the Greek term παρακλητον (*parakleton*), meaning "intercessor, counselor, advocate, comforter." He "is the one summoned, called to one's side esp. called to one's aid."[67] The term was used of a person called to defend someone in court.[68] The term was also used of a general helper. The gist of the term is that this advocate will be someone who has your back, is there to help guide, protect, and empower you.

God's Holy Spirit convicts us of sin and brings us to, or closer to, Christ, which leads to more Christlikeness in our lives.

> When he [the Holy Spirit] comes, he will prove the world to be in the wrong about sin and righteousness and judgment: about sin, because people do not believe in me [Jesus]; about righteousness, because I am going to the Father, where you can see me no longer; and about judgment, because the prince of this world now stands condemned. (Jn.16:8–11)

Once people realize the nature and consequence of their sin and the offer of hope that comes from Christ, they will typically want to commit to Christ and become a part of the family of God. This is for Christians too. We all need to understand, feel the remorse, and commit more fully to God through Christ, which then brings relief. Even as Christians we have varying degrees of belief and faith. Little by little we become more like Christ. God's Holy Spirit is an important part of this process.

One aspect of the work of the Holy Spirit might be described as parallel

---

[67] Παρακλητον. *New Strongs Dictionary*, Ibid., §3875, 1291.

[68] *Advocate*. Bible Study Tools at https://www.biblestudytools.com/dictionary/advocate/.

to that of the Bible—to lead people into truth and thus a knowledge of Christ (Jn.16:13). All scripture is inspired by God and the result of people who "spoke from God as they were carried along by the Holy Spirit" (2Pe.1:21). His Spirit was active in the creation of scripture. As such, the message of the Bible and the message from the Holy Spirit within should not be in conflict. They both come from the same personage of God's Trinity.

The Spirit helps us live the abundant, victorious Christian life. Jesus told the disciples the Holy Spirit "will teach you all things and will remind you of everything I have said to you" (Jn.14:26). He brought comfort to those not certain they would have the right words to say in a difficult situation, advising "do not worry about how you will defend yourselves or what you will say, for the Holy Spirit will teach you at that time what you should say" (Lk.12:11–12). Jesus told his disciples the Holy Spirit would glorify Christ (Jn.16:14). "Glorify" translates the Greek term δοξαζω (*doxazo*), which means "magnify, extol, or praise."[69] It is a term that refers to the promotion of the true brilliance of he who is being glorified. The truth will hold up and set apart Christ, the Savior of the world. The Spirit will help us see the true wonder of Christ and what he has done for us.

God's Holy Spirit calls us to ministry. Paul's world had been turned upside down when Christ confronted him on the road to Damascus (Ac.9). Over the next several years, Paul grew and matured with the help of other dedicated Christians, like Barnabas. At the right time, God called Paul and Barnabas to what would become Paul's primary lifetime ministry.

> While they were worshiping the Lord and fasting, the Holy Spirit said, "Set apart for me Barnabas and Saul for the work to which I have called them." So after they had fasted and prayed, they placed their hands on them and sent them off. (Ac.13:2–3)

Most full-time ministers and missionaries have heard this call of the Holy Spirit, and their lifetime of service is the result of answering the call.

---

[69] *Glorify*. James Strong, *The New Strong's Expanded Dictionary of Bible Words* (Nashville: Thomas Nelson Publishers, 2001), 1050, §1392.

The Imagery of the Holy Spirit

God's Holy Spirit is depicted as several different familiar images. Each of these images tells us something about who the Holy Spirit is.

1. *Water.* God's Spirit is pictured as water, a source of endless refreshment.

   Jesus answered, "Everyone who drinks this water will be thirsty again, but whoever drinks the water I give them will never thirst. Indeed, the water I give them will become in them a spring of water welling up to eternal life." (Jn.4:13–14)

   Whoever believes in me, as Scripture has said, rivers of living water will flow from within them." By this he meant the Spirit, whom those who believed in him were later to receive. (Jn.7:38–39)

2. *Dove.* God's Holy Spirit is portrayed as a dove, a sign of peace coming down from heaven.

   As soon as Jesus was baptized, he went up out of the water. At that moment heaven was opened, and he saw the Spirit of God descending like a dove and alighting on him. (Mt.3:16)

3. *Wind.* God's Spirit is unpredictable and moves freely over this world and in our lives.

   When the day of Pentecost came, they were all together in one place. Suddenly a sound like the blowing of a violent wind came from heaven and filled the whole house where they were sitting. (Ac.2:1–2)

   The wind blows wherever it pleases. You hear its sound, but you cannot tell where it comes from or where it is going. So it is with everyone born of the Spirit." (Jn.3:8)

4. *Fire.* God's Spirit is a flame that ignites the human soul. As the disciples gathered together to wait for something to happen, the Holy Spirit blew around them.

They saw what seemed to be tongues of fire that separated and came to rest on each of them. All of them were filled with the Holy Spirit and began to speak in other tongues as the Spirit enabled them. (Ac.2:3–4)

It was the pillar of fire by night that gave Moses and his followers the direction they needed to find their way to the promised land (Ex.13:21), and it is God's Holy Spirit today that provides Christians with the light of direction through life's challenges.

Power of the Holy Spirit

This Holy Spirit is like the current that runs through an electrical appliance in that he is the power behind our Christian lives and ministries. Spiritual gifts come from the Holy Spirit (Ro.12; 1Co.12). Our change in perspective comes largely from the Holy Spirit (1Co.2). Victory in life comes through the work of the Holy Spirit (Ro.8). God's Holy Spirit shapes and changes us. Paul provides us with words of encouragement about the Spirit's power. "May the God of hope fill you with all joy and peace as you trust in him, so that you may overflow with hope by the power of the Holy Spirit" (Ro.15:13).

Thought Questions

1. How do you imagine the Holy Spirit?
2. In what ways is the Holy Spirit a part of God?
3. What work of the Holy Spirit is really important to you?
4. What image of the Holy Spirit is most meaningful to you?
5. In what ways does the Holy Spirit bring you closer to the abundant, victorious Christian life?

CHAPTER ELEVEN

Coming of the Holy Spirit

Before the Outpouring of the Spirit

God's Spirit has been active since the beginning of time. Genesis 1 begins at the creation of the world, referencing the presence of God's Spirit.

> In the beginning God created the heavens and the earth. Now the earth was formless and empty, darkness was over the surface of the deep, and the *Spirit* of God was hovering over the waters. (Gen.1:1–2)

We can see God's Spirit at work throughout the Old Testament. God's Spirit would temporarily alight upon someone of God's choosing to empower that servant to undertake some important work. God's Spirit might reside with the servant for only an evening, or he might reside with the servant for years. The length of time depended on the needs of the person whom God was empowering to carry out the work.

One example of how God used his Spirit to temporarily empower people for specific works can be found in the life of Moses. In Moses's day, God decided to empower some of the elders to share in the work of building up the nation of Israel.

> So Moses went out and told the people what the LORD had said. He brought together seventy of their elders and had them stand around the tent. Then the LORD came

down in the cloud and spoke with him, and he took some
of the *power of the Spirit* that was on him and put it on
the seventy elders. When *the Spirit* rested on them, they
prophesied—but did not do so again. (Nu.11:24–25)

Upon receiving the Spirit, the elders began to proclaim the Word of
God. But notice this was not a giving that empowered the elders to *continue*
prophesying. They did this once and then "did not do so again." The gift
of the Spirit on these elders was not permanent. God poured out his Spirit
for a specific work.

The Spirit came upon Saul, who then prophesied, but only for a
limited time (1Sa.10:10–13). Later, the Spirit of the Lord came upon Saul
again to empower him to rescue the City of Jabesh (1Sa.11:6). Then the
Spirit is expressly described as departing from Saul in 1 Samuel 16:14.[70]

God poured out his Spirit on many others, but not upon all the people
of God. The gift of the Holy Spirit was given to empower individuals for
specific works of God. When Balaam was confronted with a spiritual
challenge, the Spirit was sent to empower him and he began to prophesy
(Nu.24:2). The Spirit of the Lord came upon Othniel, a judge, to empower
him to challenge the rule of the Aram Naharaim (Jdg.3:10). The Spirit
came upon Gideon, who rescued God's people from the Midianites and
Amalekites (Jdg.6:34). The Spirit of the Lord came upon Samson to
empower him to confront the Philistines (Jdg.14:6).

The Spirit also came upon David (1Sa.16:13). In David's prayer of
repentance to God after Nathan confronted him with his sin of adultery
and murder, David pled with God. "Do not cast me from your presence or
take your *Holy Spirit* from me" (Ps.51:11). God had given David his Spirit
and David was asking that the Spirit not be taken from him because of his
sin. He knew God's Spirit was his strength and power of rule. He knew
God's Spirit was not something he wanted to lose. And he knew sin could
really mess things up. God knew David had stumbled, but also knew that
David was a man of great faith.

---

[70] *Spirit came upon Saul.* The Bible also speaks of an evil spirit that came from the
Lord that tormented Saul (1Sa.16:14). Whenever this occurred, David would play
his harp and calm Saul (1Sa.16:23).

Pointing to Jesus

Some seven centuries before the birth and baptism of Jesus, God spoke through the prophet Isaiah about the coming Messiah. Isaiah was called to be a prophet of God through visions he received while serving in the Jerusalem Temple about 740 BCE (Isa.6). Isaiah prophesied about how God would put his Spirit on the coming Messiah (Isa.42:1). Later the prophet spoke as if the Messiah himself was speaking through him.

> The Spirit of the Sovereign LORD is on me, because the LORD has anointed me to proclaim good news to the poor. He has sent me to bind up the brokenhearted, to proclaim freedom for the captives and release from darkness for the prisoners, to proclaim the year of the LORD's favor and the day of vengeance of our God, to comfort all who mourn. (Isa.61:1–2)

In approximately 7 to 4 BCE, Jesus was born and laid in a manger. Pursuant to custom, on the eighth day after the birth, Joseph and Mary brought the baby Jesus to the Jerusalem Temple for circumcision and purification.

> Now there was a man in Jerusalem called Simeon, who was righteous and devout. He was waiting for the consolation of Israel, and the Holy Spirit was on him. It had been revealed to him by the *Holy Spirit* that he would not die before he had seen the Lord's Messiah. *Moved by the Spirit,* he went into the temple courts. When the parents brought in the child Jesus to do for him what the custom of the Law required, Simeon took him in his arms and praised God. (Lk.2:25–28)

The Holy Spirit revealed and then moved Simeon that day. I wonder what Simeon was doing when he was "moved by the Spirit" to get up and go into the temple courts? Was it just a restlessness on a lazy day or a sharp burst of energy that got him moving? Was it a quiet voice that said, "Go!" Whatever it felt or looked like, we know that God's Spirit first prepared

Simeon for what was to come and then nudged and led him to the baby Jesus.

Given to Jesus

As a grown man about thirty years of age, Jesus prepared for the start of his public ministry by going to John the Baptist to be baptized by him. John reluctantly consented because he thought Jesus should be baptizing him instead of the other way around. But it was at this time that John saw the Holy Spirit come down upon Jesus and provide John with the understanding that Jesus was the Messiah.

> As soon as Jesus was baptized, he went up out of the water. At that moment heaven was opened, and he saw *the Spirit of God* descending like a dove and alighting on him. And a voice from heaven said, "This is my Son, whom I love; with him I am well pleased." (Mt.3:16-17) [See also Jn.1:32–34]

As soon as Jesus took the step of commitment to God's leadership symbolized by baptism, God blessed him by pouring out his Holy Spirit upon him.

Following his baptism, Jesus went into the wilderness to overcome the temptations of Satan. After forty days in the wilderness, Jesus began his public ministry in a Nazareth synagogue, where he spoke the words Isaiah had written seven centuries before and applied them to himself and the Spirit's power accompanied him (Lk.4:14–15).

> "The *Spirit of the Lord* is on me, because he has anointed me to proclaim good news to the poor. He has sent me to proclaim freedom for the prisoners and recovery of sight for the blind, to set the oppressed free, to proclaim the year of the Lord's favor." Then he rolled up the scroll, gave it back to the attendant and sat down. The eyes of everyone in the synagogue were fastened on him. He began by saying to them, "Today this scripture is fulfilled in your hearing." (Lk.4:18–21)

God's Spirit had been poured out on Jesus to empower him for the unique and challenging ministry he'd been given. He would need that empowering because his ministry would not be easy.

The Holy Spirit at Work in the Church

Luke's writing, known as Acts, focused on the first three decades of the church. It is sometimes deemed the *Acts of the Holy Spirit* because the Spirit is so vividly described as the force behind the growth of the church.[71] Luke explained that Jesus gave instructions to the apostles "through the Holy Spirit" (Ac.1:1–2). We don't know the logistics of how this worked, but the Holy Spirit was part of the process that Jesus used to make known his final instructions to the apostles. The Spirit then continued to work in the early church after Jesus ascended to heaven. "Living in the fear of the Lord and encouraged by the *Holy Spirit*, it increased in numbers" (Ac.9:31).

It was the Spirit of God who helped people like Peter understand that the church was not just for Jews. Once the apostle Peter had a vision of a sheet coming down from heaven with different animals on it (Ac.10). Some were clean and some were unclean as identified by the Old Testament (Lev.11). In this vision, God instructed Peter to eat from them all, as if there were no more unclean animals.

> While Peter was still thinking about the vision, the *Spirit* said to him, "Simon, three men are looking for you. So get up and go downstairs. Do not hesitate to go with them, for I have sent them." (Ac.10:19–20)

Peter went and found himself at the house of Cornelius, a Gentile. Gentiles were deemed unclean to the orthodox Jew and Peter would not have been able to fully interact with Cornelius under the traditions of the Jewish faith. Peter proclaimed to Cornelius and his household that Jesus was empowered by the Holy Spirit to illustrate that Jesus's ministry was from God (Ac.10:37–38). Then the Holy Spirit was poured out on

---

[71] *Acts of the Holy Spirit.* Wikipedia. "Holy Spirit in the Acts of the Apostles." https://en.wikipedia.org/wiki/Holy_Spirit_in_the_Acts_of_the_Apostles. Publ. June 7, 2019.

Cornelius and his household and they began to speak in tongues and to praise God (Ac.10:44–46). It was at that point that Peter understood that Gentiles should not be deemed "unclean." God's Spirit had been engaged in this process of leading Peter to this breakthrough perspective.

The church leaders were told by the Holy Spirit to send Barnabas and Saul (aka Paul) out to share the good news of Jesus Christ (Ac.13:1–3). God's Spirit was with the church and led the church. Without God's Holy Spirit, the church would just be a bunch of people trying to do something on their own power. With God's Holy Spirit, the church was, and is, a group of people infused with the power and mind of Christ.

The Promise of the Outpouring to All

Throughout the Old Testament God sent his Spirit to empower individuals or groups for particular ministry tasks, but the Spirit remained with the individual or group only until God's task was completed. Following the birth of the church, God would continue this practice with spiritual gifting. Through spiritual gifting God empowered individuals to carry out one or more ministry tasks. But additionally, something new and different came with the birth of the church that had not been seen before the coming of Jesus. God announced this as the outpouring of the Holy Spirit. In the latter days of the Old Testament prophets, God spoke through Joel, saying, "I will pour out my Spirit on all people. Your sons and daughters will prophesy, your old men will dream dreams, your young men will see visions" (Joel 2:28).

John the Baptist was the forerunner for Jesus and announced his coming, along with the promise of the Holy Spirit.

> "I baptize you with water for repentance. But after me comes one who is more powerful than I, whose sandals I am not worthy to carry. He will baptize you with the Holy Spirit and fire. (Mt.3:11)

After the resurrection but before the ascension to heaven, Jesus told his disciples, "I am going to send you what my Father has promised; but stay in the city until you have been clothed with power from on high" (Lk.24:49).

Although God's people knew something new was coming in the way of the Holy Spirit, nobody was really sure what that would look like. They had to wait for God's outpouring to occur to understand it. They found out when the Spirit was poured out on the infant church in Jerusalem.

Given to Believers

God's Holy Spirit is given to *all* believers who commit their lives to God through Christ. The promise was given in the first Christian sermon by Peter. Following the ascension of Jesus into heaven after his resurrection, God poured out his Spirit on a group of disciples of Jesus who were huddled in an upper room uncertain what to do next. They were waiting for that "power from on high" that Jesus had referenced. Suddenly there was the sound of a violent wind, the visual appearance of tongues of fire over the heads of the disciples, and then the disciples began speaking in tongues[72] as the Spirit enabled them. A crowd of pilgrims from many countries just outside the room heard this strange commotion and gathered to listen. What they heard astounded them. They heard these Galilean disciples speaking in the pilgrim's own native languages (Ac.2). Peter took the lead and explained what was going on to all who were present. When the people understood that the Messiah had come and died for them, they asked what they should do.

> Peter replied, "Repent and be baptized, every one of you,
> in the name of Jesus Christ for the forgiveness of your sins.
> And you will receive the gift of the Holy Spirit. (Ac.2:38)

The promise was announced that if one committed his or her life to God through Christ, that person's sins would be forgiven and he or she would receive the gift of the Holy Spirit. Anyone who chose to commit would have the gift of the Holy Spirit. This was very different than how God poured out his Spirit in the Old Testament on select individuals or small groups of people for specific ministry tasks.

---

[72] *Speaking in tongues.* The description here indicates that these Galilean disciples, who would not have typically known the languages of the pilgrims, were being heard by the pilgrims in the pilgrims' own languages. Clearly this was a miracle empowered through the working of the Holy Spirit.

Given without Limit

At one point, John's disciples were concerned because Jesus's disciples had also begun baptizing. John assuaged their worry and explained, "For the one whom God has sent speaks the words of God, for *God gives the Spirit without limit*" (Jn.3:34).

There are two different interpretations of the phrase "God gives the Spirit without limit." Some view this as a reference to the Spirit who was poured out on Jesus. Jesus was given the Spirit "without limit." The Greek words translated "without limit" are ου γαρ (*ou gar* = without) and μετρον (*metron* = measure). *Ou gar* is simply a common phrase meaning "contrary to." Thus our English translations translate the Greek as "without." *Metron* refers to some ability to measure the degree in virtually any context. You don't need to measure the degree if the degree is full. Here, the Son was given the Spirit without any limit or measure. Jesus received God's Holy Spirit in full, without any limitations.[73]

Jesus had the full measure of the Holy Spirit without limit in time, range, or role. He allowed God's Spirit to work fully within and through him and was empowered to carry out the ministry God had given the Son here on earth. As such, in Jesus we see bold preaching, wisdom in the words spoken, the power of healing, the strength of courage, and the peace that surpasses all understanding.

And yet it may be that God gives the Spirit without limit to all believers who commit to Christ. God doesn't dole out his Spirit in portions. He gives all of himself to each one of us who has committed to him. Our only limitations are in the way we open ourselves to God's working within and through us. We can grieve (Eph.4:29–32), quench, (1Thes.5:19), or resist (Ac.7:51) the Holy Spirit by refusing to allow God to lead. Or we can allow God's Spirit to fully guide us and take us wherever God wants us to be. We want the spiritual current from God to flow unhindered.

---

[73] *Speaking of Jesus.* The context of this passage shows a focus on Jesus Christ. As such, it would appear reasonable that John is speaking of Jesus in making this statement.

Thought Questions

1. What did those in the Old Testament lack in the working of the Holy Spirit that we have today?
2. Why is the indwelling Holy Spirit so important to us?
3. In what ways do the Old Testament prophecies about God's Spirit reveal his plan?
4. How much do you think those who made the prophecies about God's coming Holy Spirit understood about what was coming?
5. What does it mean to you that God gives the Holy Spirit without limit?

CHAPTER TWELVE

The Holy Spirit Inside

The Coming Holy Spirit

Although the Holy Spirit had temporarily alighted on people to empower them for some specific ministry task in the past, a new way of giving the Holy Spirit would come after the crucifixion and resurrection of Jesus. While in Jerusalem, prior to his arrest, Jesus spoke to the crowd about the coming Holy Spirit who would quench the spiritual thirst of the people.

> On the last and greatest day of the festival, Jesus stood and said in a loud voice, "Let anyone who is thirsty come to me and drink. Whoever believes in me, as Scripture has said, rivers of living water will flow from within them." By this he meant the Spirit, whom those who believed in him were later to receive. Up to that time the Spirit had not been given, since Jesus had not yet been glorified. (Jn.7:37–39)

Notice Jesus said just before his arrest that this living water would flow "from within." There was something different that was coming. This power didn't touch individuals from some outside force. Rather something or someone would transform humankind from the inside out. Although he didn't explain it in any detail, Jesus was giving the people a hint as to how this new coming of the Spirit would work.

Later he explained more clearly that there is a difference between those who commit to Jesus and those who do not. It's a difference in the way they see and understand. There is a difference of perspective that can only come from the Spirit.

> "If you love me, keep my commands. And I will ask the Father, and he will give you another advocate to help you and be with you forever—the Spirit of truth. The world cannot accept him, because it neither sees him nor knows him. But you know him, for *he lives with you and will be in you.* (Jn.14:15–17)

Just before being carried up into heaven to sit at the right hand of the father, Jesus gathered with his disciples and said:

> You are witnesses of these things. I am going to send you what my Father has promised; but stay in the city until you have been clothed with power from on high." (Lk.24:48–49)

What was this promised "power from on high?" Perhaps the disciples were thinking of something like the parting of the sea in the days of Moses. Or maybe it would be the smoke, lightning, and thunder from the top of Mount Sinai. When we think of power, we tend to think of those big acts that hold us in awe.

The Outpouring

The outpouring of the Holy Spirit prophesied by the prophet Joel would not occur until Jesus had been glorified (Jn.7:37–39). The glorification of Jesus came with the death, burial, and resurrection of Jesus. It is easy to see how the resurrection glorified Christ. The resurrection displayed the divine power over life and death. This is a power no one can duplicate. It's a power that overcomes even death itself to bring victory in life. Yet it was the night of torture and death on the cross that showed us the depth of Christ's love for us. Here is where Christ's love for people was on full display. Here is where we learn how far Christ will go to save the people he loves. The glorification, which truly revealed the brilliance of Jesus Christ to the world, was that powerful message of love and power bookended by the crucifixion and the resurrection. This is what Paul says was of first importance (1Co.15:3–5).

The disciples were to wait in Jerusalem until they received the "power from on high" (Lk.24:48–49). The disciples didn't have to wait long. It happened at the festival of Pentecost, the Greek term for the Jewish Feast of Weeks. This feast came on the fiftieth day after the first Sabbath of the Passover Feast.[74] Since Jesus was raised on the day after the first Sabbath of the Feast, Pentecost would therefore have fallen fifty days after the resurrection of Jesus.

> When the day of Pentecost came, they were all together in one place. Suddenly a sound like the blowing of a violent wind came from heaven and filled the whole house where they were sitting. They saw what seemed to be tongues of fire that separated and came to rest on each of them. All of them were filled with the Holy Spirit and began to speak in other tongues as the Spirit enabled them. (Ac.2:1–4)

Those who witnessed this strange sight were confused. They came from many different lands. They were watching and hearing these uneducated Galileans speak in the hearers' foreign languages. How could these disciples, with limited regional experience and training, be speaking in languages of far-off lands? As the confusion grew from this spectacle, the apostle Peter rose and addressed the crowds that had gathered. He explained that this was the outpouring of the Holy Spirit that the prophet Joel had predicted (Ac.2:16[75]). This event with the sounds of wind, the vision of flames over the heads of the people, and the speaking in tongues got the people's attention so that Peter could explain that everyone who committed to God through Christ would receive the gift of the Holy Spirit (Ac.2:38). Something new and amazing had happened. God was infusing his people with his Spirit in a new way.

This is the Holy Spirit coming to live *within* each and every committed believer for as long as that believer remains faithful to Christ. This indwelling

---

[74] *Fiftieth day.* Lev.23:16; Dt.16:9.
[75] *Predicted by Joel.* Joel 2:28–32.

Holy Spirit is so important to the Christian that the apostle Paul points out that if you don't have the Spirit within, you don't belong to Christ (Ro.8:9).

Transformation

The indwelling Holy Spirit is part of God's process to change us day by day into people of Christlike nature. Upon committing to Christ, God's Holy Spirit is given to dwell within us permanently. God's Spirit then intermeshes with ours, and we begin to see things in a new light with a new Christlike perspective. Paul said it this way:

> The person without the Spirit does not accept the things that come from the Spirit of God but considers them foolishness, and cannot understand them because they are discerned only through the Spirit ... for, "Who has known the mind of the Lord so as to instruct him?" But we have the mind of Christ. (1Co.2:14–16)

Because God's Holy Spirit lives within us, the mind of Christ also lives within us. To the degree that we allow God's Spirit to direct and guide us, we slowly become Christlike in nature. It is a gradual transformation of allowing God's Holy Spirit more and more control in our lives.

Gives Life

The indwelling Holy Spirit gives life to the Christian (Jn.6:63; 2Co.3:6; 1Pe.3:18). He changes our attitudes. Allowing the Spirit to lead quite naturally bears Christian traits. Paul describes this process as parallel to the way fruit grows on a tree. A healthy fruit tree will naturally grow its particular type of fruit. A Spirit-filled soul will naturally grow certain traits in life. "The fruit of the Spirit is love, joy, peace, forbearance, kindness, goodness, faithfulness, gentleness and self-control" (Gal.5:22–23). The full and abundant life includes these lifestyle characteristics. They are ours to the degree we open ourselves to the Holy Spirit's guidance and power.

Additionally, this indwelling Spirit is our sign of being a Christian that guarantees our eternal future with our Lord. When you buy a house or car through financing, you put down a deposit to the seller as proof that you will make the purchase. Spiritually, God is buying our souls, and he puts down the Spirit as a deposit to confirm that he will make the purchase.

> When you believed, you were marked in him with a seal, the promised Holy Spirit, who is a deposit guaranteeing our inheritance until the redemption of those who are God's possession—to the praise of his glory. (Eph.1:13–14)

God's Holy Spirit becomes the power by which we are raised to new life (Ro.8:11). He is our spiritual current. He is what empowers us to live the Christian life.

Filled with the Holy Spirit

When one is fully open to the Holy Spirit's guidance, he or she is said to be "full of the Holy Spirit." John the Baptist experienced this complete filling. At his birth, John's father was told John "will be great in the sight of the Lord. He is never to take wine or other fermented drink, and he will be *filled with the Holy Spirit* even before he is born" (Lk.1:15). As an adult, John boldly proclaimed the message that people should repent for the coming of the messiah (Lk.3:3–20). It is this boldness in proclaiming the message of God that is common in all who are "filled with the Holy Spirit."

After his baptism, Jesus went "full of the Holy Spirit" into the wilderness for forty days (Lk.4:1). He was "led by the Spirit" into the desert (Lk.4:1). With great courage and will, Jesus faced down the devil by boldly proclaiming God's Word in response to every enticement.

When the first Christians began to speak in languages not their own, it was the Spirit boldly empowering them to preach the Word of God to those who would not have otherwise understood the message (Ac.2:4). Later, Peter and John were brought before the Sanhedrin, the local Jewish ruling council. "Filled with the Holy Spirit," they boldly spoke the Word of God to the Jews who were persecuting them for presenting such a message (Ac.4:8). God's Spirit had empowered them with the courage and words to proclaim God's message in a hostile environment. Even when they were warned not to teach about Jesus, they continued to do so. "After they prayed, the place where they were meeting was shaken. And they were all *filled with the Holy Spirit* and *spoke the word of God boldly*" (Ac.4:31).

A number of early Christians were described as being full of the Holy Spirit. Stephen was arrested and brought before the Jewish rulers, where he made his defense by boldly proclaiming God's message. It is said he was "filled with the Holy Spirit" (Ac.7:55). Barnabas, the great encourager, was said to be a good man "full of the Holy Spirit" and faith. It was because of this that he was able to bring many people to Christ—presumably by boldly speaking to people about Jesus (Ac.11:24). The apostle Paul was "filled with the Holy Spirit." When he met the sorcerer Elymas, he boldly and sharply confronted him in the name of God (Ac.13:9–11).

It is pretty clear that being "filled with the Holy Spirit" means two things. (1) The person who is filled has sought to be led by God (Lk.4:1). (2) The result is the bold proclamation of God's message (Lk.1:15; 4:1; Ac.2:4; 4:8, 31; 7:55; 11:24; 13:9, 52). The Spirit empowers one to share the good news of Jesus Christ boldly with others.

Resisting the Holy Spirit

The Holy Spirit can fill each of us if we allow ourselves to be fully open to God's guidance and empowerment. On the other hand, we can also limit the Spirit's effectiveness. Stephen, the first Christian martyr, addressed the Jews who had rejected Christ and were persecuting Christians and alleged, "You always *resist* the Holy Spirit!" (Ac.7:51). Perhaps this resisting is refusing to go where the Spirit leads, refusing to say the words the Spirit places in your mind, refusing to look for God's guidance in the situation, or refusal to treat marginalized people with real love and care. God doesn't use his power to overwhelm a person's individual will. We have the capability of resisting.

Our lifestyles can also grieve the Holy Spirit. The apostle Paul lays out behavior for us to follow in order to avoid that:

> And do not *grieve* the Holy Spirit of God, with whom you were sealed for the day of redemption. Get rid of all bitterness, rage and anger, brawling and slander, along with every form of malice. Be kind and compassionate to one another, forgiving each other, just as in Christ God forgave you. (Eph.4:29–32, see also Isa.63:10)

As Christians, we are the people of God, living a life that mirrors the values of Christ and opening ourselves to the guidance and empowerment of the Holy Spirit. In so doing, we will experience the filling of the Holy Spirit and the true power that only God can provide to help in our development and in carrying out the ministries he has given us.

God's Spirit is the power that enables us to live the Christian life. He is the one who provides us with the ability to view life through God's eyes. God's Spirit is the current that runs through us when we are fully plugged into to God.

Thought Questions

1. What do you think the Christians felt and thought as the Holy Spirit was poured out on them in Acts 2?
2. Did you feel a difference or change at the time you committed your life to Christ? What kind of difference?
3. What does God's Holy Spirit bring to your life?
4. Do you sense there is a gradual and growing change in your life as you open up to God's guidance? Describe that process.
5. Do you pray to be filled with God's Holy Spirit? Why?

Epilogue

The Power of Transformation

The power of God is revealed in many forms. God has parted the sea to allow the Hebrews to escape slavery in Egypt. He has healed those with debilitating diseases. He has even brought the dead to life. But the greatest effect of his power is not in any of these wonders. It is God's transforming power in our own lives that has the most and deepest meaning of all. The prophet Ezekiel promised something to God's people that outshines all other acts of God:

> I will give them an undivided heart and put a new spirit in them; I will remove from them their heart of stone and give them a heart of flesh. Then they will follow my decrees and be careful to keep my laws. They will be my people, and I will be their God. (Ez.11:19–20)

Gordon MacDonald provides twelve characteristics of a Christian transformed by God. "1. Has an undiluted devotion to Jesus. 2. Pursues a biblically informed view of the world. 3. Is intentional and disciplined in seeking God's direction in life. 4. Worships and has a spirit of continuous repentance. 5. Builds healthy, reciprocal human relationships. 6. Knows how to engage the larger world where faith is not necessarily understood. 7. Is aware of personal "call" and unique competencies. 8. Is merciful and generous. 9. Appreciates that suffering is part of faithfulness to Jesus. 10.

Is eager and ready to express the content of his faith. 11. Overflows with thankfulness. 12. Has a passion for reconciliation."[76]

The apostle Paul points out that this transformation begins with a transformation of the mind (Ro.12:2). This renewing of the mind comes from the three prongs of the spiritual plug powered by the indwelling Holy Spirit. From deep within our own souls, God's Spirit can mesh with our own and change us from the inside out. The result of this transformation by the Spirit of God is powerful.

Without and with the Power

One man provides a clear example of the difference between trying to plug into the power of God with a three-prong plug and trying to do so without all three prongs. He had been trained as a Christian leader. He was submissive to his ministry mentors, who themselves had been well trained for ministry. He was directly connected to the church. He was smart, well educated, articulate, and had literary prowess. He wanted to serve God and was honest about his own frailties and failings.

He prayed fervently, pleading for forgiveness of his shortcomings and asking God to give him victory. From morning to night, he called out to God with confession and petition. He was constantly aware of God's oversight and his heart ached for God's healing and love.

He deprived himself of the excesses that can divert one's mind and heart from God. He would not indulge in the selfish exuberances that blind one's ability to see God and his wonderful creation. He really wanted to be God's minister on earth and felt called to fulfill that role.

He fulfilled all the ritualistic practices. His church had many such rituals, and he knew them well. He taught others how to practice them. Creeds were repeated over and over. He believed that to be right with God one needed attend church at particular times to obtain ongoing forgiveness. He saw a distinction between clergy and the lay church members. The clergy were intermediaries between God and humankind. This man was part of that special class that ministers to the lay congregation.

---

[76] CT Pastors. "*How to Spot a Transformed Christian.*" Gordon MacDonald. 2012. http://www.christianitytoday.com/pastors/2012/summer/transformedchristian.html.

Yet in spite of all the rituals he performed and the service he rendered, he was tormented with the fear that he was not good enough, that God did not love him, and that he was on a trajectory that would carry him to hell instead of heaven. He had a *one* prong spiritual plug that he used to connect to God. He had prayer, but prayer alone. No matter how much he prayed, how much he deprived himself of the indulgences of life, how much he sought God, he could not find peace. He did not have an effective ministry. The harder he tried, the less confident he became that he was getting any closer to God. Even though he had been religiously trained, engaged in diligent prayer, and carried out all of his religious duties, he had no confidence that he was being held in the hands, arms, and love of God.

Over time this man came to realize that what he was doing was not working, yet he could not figure out what needed to change. Then he was asked to teach from Paul's letter to the Romans in the Bible. Of course, that meant he had to *read* Romans. Oh, he knew the creeds of his church, knew quite a bit of church history, and he knew some selected Bible passages that were included in the scripted services he led. But he had not read the Bible on any regular, consistent basis. There were large portions of the Bible he had never read. For a man trained to be a religious minister, he had a pitiful knowledge of the Bible. And so he began. Day after day, he read, reread, read with prayer, jotted notes, created a lesson plan to teach, and completely immersed himself in Paul's letter to the Romans.

It didn't take long. Working through the first chapter of Romans, he found a new perspective that he had never contemplated before.

> I felt that I had been born anew and that the gates of heaven had been opened. The whole of Scripture gained a new meaning. And from that point on the phrase, 'the justice of God' no longer filled me with hatred, but rather became unspeakable sweet by virtue of a great love.[77]

He meditated on what he read, wrestled with what he read, prayed about what he read. Then he continued on, step by step, chapter by chapter, verse by verse, through the entire book of Romans. By the time he had

---

[77] Goodreads. "Gates of Heaven." https://www.goodreads.com/quotes/878756-i-felt-that-i-had-been-born-anew-and-that.

finished his study, he was a completely different man. He was truly a new creation.

Through this Bible study, he had connected with God in a new way. He saw God as he had never seen him before. God had spoken to him through the pages of the Bible. Throughout his study, the small flame within his heart for God began to grow in size until he was spiritually on fire. Once having tasted what the study of God's Word could do, this young minister dove into the Bible with passion and continued through the rest of his life feeding on the Word of God as revealed in the Bible.

Then something else changed. Through his study of the Bible, this member of the clergy realized he needed to be *with* the people of God. Church became something completely different for him. He saw the church as the *community* of believers. There wasn't a separate class of people called "priests." Rather everyone was to be a priest (2Pe.2:9). He came to believe in the priesthood of all believers.[78] He wasn't at the church building simply to fulfill his ritualistic duties. In fact, he fought aggressively against some of the rituals he had earlier accepted that did not build the believers into a community of faith. As a leader he realized he wasn't just preaching God *at* them. He was sharing God's love *with* them. He needed to encourage and be encouraged. He needed to be tied with love to the other Christians who made up the Body of Christ—the Church. He needed to be an integral part of the body in which no one person with his or her gifts was any greater than anyone else. He became a true partner in faith with the other members.

It was on October 31, 1517, that this young priest nailed ninety-five propositional theses on the door of the Wittenberg Church in Germany to start what is known as the Reformation. As he learned how to plug into the power of God, this young minister led a movement that changed the world. His name was Martin Luther.

A Three-Prong Plug

To realize for ourselves the type of transformation we see in the life of Martin Luther or of countless others who have accessed the power of God,

---

[78] Eric Metaxas, *Martin Luther: The Man Who Rediscovered God and Changed the World* (New York: Penguin Books, 2018), 180–186.

we must first plug in. That plug is a *three*-prong spiritual plug. Martin Luther had started with a one-prong (prayer) plug, but it wasn't until he tapped into the other two that his life and ministry truly caught fire.

At one point in my life I became a serious runner. I had been invited to join a running group and decided I would train with this group and try to complete my first marathon. The training consisted of three main components: (1) hill running to develop strength, (2) track running to develop speed, (3) and ever-increasing distance running to develop stamina. Each of these training components was important to my overall development as a runner. Had I left one or more out, my running would have been handicapped.

I also needed to be consistent. I might survive skipping one week, but skipping more began to affect my strength and speed. I would not be able to run a marathon with a haphazard approach to my training. I took my training seriously and religiously followed all three components. As such, my first marathon was a tremendous experience. The victory of completing the marathon overcame any sense of fatigue. In the same way, our spiritual training comes by plugging in with this three-prong plug to connect to God.

There are times when we can't plug in with all three prongs due to conditions beyond our control. Medical professionals, police, and others sometimes need to work on Sundays. Shut-ins due to age, illness, or injury may not be able to meet with other Christians as easily as those who are healthy. Prisoners of war often find it impossible to meet with others in Christian fellowship or read the Bible. Whereas meeting together and reading the Bible are important for plugging into the power of God, it is not fatal to be unable to participate due to conditions outside of one's control. God is ready to step in and help.

However, not being able to meet or read the Bible takes its toll on the one who cannot participate in these prongs, and it makes prayer even more important. The good news is that God knows the hearts of these people who would desire to meet with other Christians and engage in Bible study but cannot. He will supply the power to make it through.

This is very different from those who simply choose not to answer the call to fully plug in. The difference is in the heart of the participant. One who loves God will do his or her best to plug in with all three prongs of the spiritual plug because that is what God wants and has encouraged us to do. The one who chooses not to plug in is letting his or her own selfish desires or fears take precedent over God's desires and help. We are called on to have faith in God and to allow him to lead.

The first prong of this spiritual plug is frequent (daily) reading of the Bible. This is the ground plug to protect us from the dangerous aspects of culture that might put us in harm's way. We study the Bible to learn about God, to learn what God wants of us, to shape our understanding, and to be reminded periodically of that which we sometimes forget. We want to develop into a people who have the Word of God planted in our souls.

The second prong is daily (constant) prayer. Prayer is our primary way of communicating with God. We speak to God with requests arising out of our concern for others and our seeking of God's direction in our lives. We listen for God's response and message of guidance, which may come in any number of ways. We need communication with God as we do with every person with whom we want to build a relationship.

The third prong is regular fellowship (partnership) with other Christians in which there can be mutual encouragement to live life for God. We encourage those who are struggling while also receiving encouragement from others when we need it. If we meet with Christians with the purpose of encouraging them, we will not be fatally disappointed by the quality of the assembly or service when it doesn't meet our own personal standards and desires.

Finally, the current (power) that runs through this plug is the Holy Spirit. The Spirit is the part of God who empowers us to live the Christlike life and accomplish the ministry tasks he gives to us. Whether the task be small or great, mundane or miraculous, it is this power of God that we need to accomplish his ministry in his way.

When we sincerely and diligently plug into God, when we close that circuit and allow the power to flow, things will happen. We will change little by little over time into what God wants us to be and find a joy and a power we never knew possible. It will happen!

> And we all, who with unveiled faces contemplate the Lord's glory, are being transformed into his image with ever-increasing glory, which comes from the Lord, who is the Spirit. (2Co.3:18)

Thought Questions

1. In what ways do you sense the transformation of God in your own life?
2. Have you ever had a time in your life where you tried to rely on less than all three prongs of the plug (Bible study, prayer, partnership with Christians)? What was that like?
3. Does the three-prong plug image help you imagine how to plug into God's power?
4. Is there another image that helps you imagine how to access the power of God? If so, describe it.
5. What have you gained from reading this book and or discussing it with friends?

SPECIAL INTEREST
BIBLE APPENDIX

Sample of the Types of Special-Interest Bibles Available

General Bibles

The Apologetics Study Bible, Holman Bible Publishers. Study notes that focus on a defense of Christianity and the reasons for belief in the subject being addressed.

The Archaeological Study Bible, Zondervan. Study notes that focus on archaeological support for the event described in the biblical passage.

The Complete Jewish Study Bible, Hendrickson Publishers Marketing, LLC. Translation and study notes that focus on the Jewish perspective of the subjects discussed in a passage.

Life Application Study Bible, Tyndale House Publishers. Includes notes that focus on making practical application of the principles being taught in the biblical passages.

The Study Bible for Women, Holman Bible Publishers. Includes notes that focus on matters that tend to interest women.

Every Man's Bible, Tyndale House Publishers. Includes notes that focus on matters that tend to interest men.

There are a host of Bibles with study notes and designs to appeal specifically to teens and to children. These are typically age referenced so that one can choose one that fits the age range of one's child.

Daily Study Bibles

The Daily Bible, Harvest House Publishers. This is one of the chronological Bibles that divides the text by chronology of events and writings rather than book by book and provides a dated daily reading plan for the text.

The One Year Bible, Tyndale House Publishers. This is a regular New Testament divided into 365 segments for daily reading with a date listed for each segment.

BIBLE MOVIE APPENDIX

Sample of Some of the Better Biblical Movies Available

1. *The Bible* (1966), directed by John Houston, is probably the best telling of the first eleven chapters of Genesis, from creation through the Tower of Babel. However, being a movie from 1966, it uses the King James Bible's seventeenth-century English "thee's" and "thou's," which influenced the way many English-speaking Christians prayed in the early 1960s.

2. *Abraham* (1993), one of the Ted Turner Entertainment biblical films in the Bible Collection, is probably the best movie about the life of Abraham beginning in Genesis 12.

3. Ted Turner also has films about the lives of later patriarchs entitled *Jacob* (1994) and *Joseph* (1995) that are well made.

4. There are a number of films made about the life of Moses— none of which are completely in concert with the descriptions in the Bible. There is the famous Charlton Heston film *The Ten Commandments* (1956), which takes certain Hollywood liberties but is a powerful telling of the story. There is also a newer movie by the same name, *The Ten Commandments* (2006), which is more accurate than the Heston film, but still includes some additions that go well beyond the text of the Bible. Ted Turner has a low-budget but relatively accurate film entitled *Moses* (1995) featuring Ben Kingsley as Moses.

5. There is an old 1949 film called *Samson and Delilah*, a 1961 Turner film called *Samson*, and a 2018 film. The first two have inaccuracies but capture the primary story of the ancient strong

man. The third is a bit more accurate but lacks some of the excitement of the first two.

6. There are a couple of films about the life of Ruth. There is the more exciting and less accurate 1960 movie, *The Story of Ruth.* There is also the more accurate but slower 2010 movie, *The Book of Ruth.*

7. There are several films about kings Saul, David and Solomon. Turner produced films titled *David* (1997), which includes Saul, and *Solomon* (1997), about first three monarchs of Israel, which are probably the best overall films about the trio. There is Richard Gere's 1985 film *King David*, which is the best depiction of Goliath as a real giant but also depicts some of the racier parts of the events.

8. Turner produced the films *Jeremiah* (1998) and *Esther* (1999), which are worth watching. The Jeremiah film adds in a Hollywood romance that isn't found in the Bible or history, but the film is still well made.

9. There is a 2013 film entitled *Daniel*, with Robert Miano.

10. There are a number of decent films about Jesus, including, (a) *The Nativity* (2006); (b) *Jesus of Nazareth* (1977); (c) the 1979 *Jesus* film, which is the only Jesus film shot in the Holy Lands near the actual historical sites; (d) a film made for TV (2010) called *Jesus*; (e) a word-for-word *Gospel of Matthew* (1995) made by Visual Bible; and (f) a word-for-word *Gospel of John* (2003) also made by Visual Bible.

11. Visual Bible produced a movie called the *Book of Acts* (1994), which tells the story of the early church. This film dramatizes the book of Acts in the word-for-word format. The story is also told in a movie titled *Peter and Paul* (1981) that stars Anthony Hopkins as Paul.

12. There is even a depiction of the apostle John receiving his revelation on the Isle of Patmos and writing the book of Revelation in a movie called *The Apocalypse* (2002), starring Richard Harris.

13. There are a number of children's films that typically insert fictional characters and may add singing to help the children engage. *Veggie Tales* is a well-known and popular series.

GREAT PRAYER APPENDIX

Sample of Some of the Prayers of Faith in the Bible

Abraham for Sodom: Gen.18:22–33

Jacob at Peniel: Gen.32:24–30

Moses requesting God not destroy his people: Nu.14:10–20

Hannah's prayer for a son: 1Sa.1:9–28

David when denied the privilege of building the temple: 2 Sam.7:18–29

Solomon at Gibeon: 1 Ki.3:6–10

Solomon at dedication of the temple: 1 Ki.8:22–53

Elijah at Carmel: 1 Ki.18:36–38

Hezekiah at the invasion of Sennacherib: 2 Ki.19:14–19; 1 Chron.17:16–27

David's prayer for repentance: Ps.51

Hezekiah when sick: Isa.38:1–3

Ezra for the sins of the people: Ezr.9:5–15

Daniel for the captive Jews: Dan.9:4–19

Habakkuk's prayer: Hab.3

Mary's prayer of thanksgiving: Lk.1:46–55

The Lord's model prayer: Mt.6:9–13

The tax collector: Lk.18:9–14

Jesus on the cross: Lk.23:34

The dying thief: Lk.23:42

Christ's intercessory prayer: Jn.17

Stephen: Ac.7:59–60

Paul for the Ephesians: Eph.3:14–21

References

Bibles

Archaeological Study Bible. Grand Rapids: The Zondervan Corporation, 2005.

The Apologetics Study Bible. Nashville: Holman Bible Publishers, 2007.

The Complete Jewish Study Bible. Peabody: Hendrickson Publishers, Marketing, LLC, 2016.

The Daily Bible. Eugene: Harvest House Publishers, 1984.

The NIV Study Bible. Grand Rapids: The Zondervan Corporation, 1985.

Stringfellow, Alan. *Through the Bible in One Year.* New Kensington: Whitaker House Publishers, 2014.

WordSearchBible11, v.11.0.8, Software, Copyright Codeweavers, Inc., 2016.

Books

Boice, James Montgomery. *Foundations of the Christian Faith.* Downers Grove: InterVarsity Press, 1986.

Bruce, F. F. *The Canon of Scripture.* Downers Grove: InterVarsity Press, 1988.

Cloninger, Claire, *101 Most Powerful Prayers in the Bible,* New York: Warner Faith, 2003.

Fee, Gordon D. and Douglas Stuart. *How to Read the Bible for All Its Worth*. Grand Rapids: Zondervan, 2014.

Garrison, Alton. *A Spirit-Empowered Church*. Springfield: Influence Resources, 2015.

Hendricks, Howard G., and William D. Hendricks. *Living by the Book*. Chicago: Moody Publishers, 2007.

Horn, David. *Soulmates*. MA: Hendrickson Publishers Marketing, LLC, 2017.

How We Got the Bible. Torrance: Rose Publishing, 2005.

Lang, J. Stephen. *The Bible on the Big Screen*. Grand Rapids: Baker Books, 2007.

Lightfoot, Neil R. *How We Got the Bible*. Grand Rapids: Baker Book House, 1983.

Metaxas, Eric. *Martin Luther: The Man Who Rediscovered God and Changed the World*. New York: Penguin Books, 2018.

Metzger, Bruce Manning. *The Text of the New Testament*. New York: Oxford University Press, 1968.

Omartian, Stormie. *The Power of Praying Together*. Eugene: Harvest House Publishers, 2003.

Rabey, Steve and Lois. *101 Most Powerful Prayers in the Bible*. New York: Warner Faith, 2003.

Scorgie, Glen G., Mark L. Strauss, and Steven M. Voth (eds). *The Challenge of Bible Translation*. Grand Rapids: The Zondervan Corporation, 2003.

Understanding the Holy Spirit Made Easy. Peabody: Hendrickson Publishers, Inc., 2014.

Hebrew and Greek Language Resources

Thayer, Joseph H. *Thayer's Greek-English Lexicon of the New Testament*. Peabody: Hendrickson Publishers, Inc., 2012.

The Interlinear NIV Hebrew-English Old Testament. Grand Rapids: Zondervan Publishing House, 1987.

The New Brown-Driver-Briggs-Gesenius Hebrew-English Lexicon. Peabody: Hendrickson Publishers, 1996.

Strong, James. *The New Strong's Expanded Dictionary of Bible Words*. Nashville: Thomas Nelson Publishers, 2001.

Online

Wikipedia. "Bible Translations." https://en.wikipedia.org/wiki/Bible_translations.

Crosswalk. "Prayer Quotes." http://www.crosswalk.com/faith/spiritual-life/inspiring-quotes/31-prayer-quotes-be-inspired-and-encouraged.html.

Davis, Craig. "Dating the New Testament." http://www.datingthenewtestament.com/Fathers.htm.

Wikipedia. "Fiddler on the Roof." https://en.wikipedia.org/wiki/Fiddler_on_the_Roof, 2017.

Goodreads. https://www.goodreads.com/quotes/878756-i-felt-that-i-had-been-born-anew-and-that.

Hancock, Graham. http://grahamhancock.com/phorum/read.php?4,762067, 762067.

Christianity Today. "How to Spot a Transformed Christian." Gordon MacDonald. http://www.christianitytoday.com/pastors/2012/summer/transformedchristian.html.

Mayo Clinic. https://www.mayoclinic.org/diseases-conditions/rotator-cuff-injury/symptoms-causes/syc-20350225.

CPSIA information can be obtained
at www.ICGtesting.com
Printed in the USA
FSHW011712130919
61993FS